Kitchen
Garden Estate

Kitchen Garden Estate

Helene Gammack

 National Trust

For Peter

An English 18th-century watercolour of Sheffield Park, Sussex, by an unknown artist. The view across the lake towards the house shows deer in the trees and people on the edge of the lake.

First published in the United Kingdom in 2012 by
National Trust Books
10 Southcombe Street
London W14 0RA
An imprint of Anova Books Ltd

ISBN: 9781907892127

A CIP catalogue record for this book is available from the British Library.

20 19 18 17 16 15 14 13 12
10 9 8 7 6 5 4 3 2 1

Reproduction by Rival Colour Ltd, UK
Printed by 1010 International Printing Ltd, China

This book can be ordered direct from the publisher at the website: www.anovabooks.com, or try your local bookshop. Also available at National Trust shops, including shop.nationaltrust.org.uk.

'... there is ... a large deer park with many deer and does, woods, a rabbit warren in the hills, and very beautiful, well kept pleasure grounds with fruit trees, well watered by a fast flowing, fresh sparkling stream of wonderfully clear, sweet water. This splits up into several branches and rivulets, also some fishponds ... There are also some vineyards round the house and gardens, producing yearly two to three hogsheads of wine. There is a dovecote like a chapel, in which are at all times so many young pigeons that throughout the whole summer and longer 12 to 14 dozen can be taken out every week and put into pies or prepared otherwise. His people go out hunting every day and catch a lot of partridges and pheasants, which we had every day on the table ... there is an ample supply of drinks, different kinds of wine and perry, which is made from pears. He also has his own brewery, bakery, wine press, hop garden, barns, stables, oxen, cows, sheep, pigs, geese, ducks, corn and fruit, everything that one can desire in such an establishment.'

WILLIAM SCHELLINK'S DESCRIPTION OF
BRIDGE PLACE, KENT (1661)

Page 2: Apple blossom in the gardens at Llanerchaeron, Ceredigion. The restored walled garden produces homegrown fruit, vegetables and herbs on the 18th-century estate.

CONTENTS

Introduction

In *The Compleat English Gentleman* (1728), Daniel Defoe described the quintessential country gentleman as having 'Venison perhaps in his park, sufficient for his own table at least, and rabbits in his own warren adjoyning, pidgeons from a dove house in the yard, fish in his own ponds or in some small river adjoyning and within his own royalty, and milk with all the needful addenda to his kitchen, which a small dairy of four or five cows yields to him'. This supply of meat and dairy produce, together with fruit and vegetables, enabled almost complete self-sufficiency and was the model for every British country estate until the industrial revolution of the 19th century.

An Bird's Eye View of Westbury Court in Gloucestershire *by Johannes Kip (c.1707). All the components of self-sufficiency can be identified.*

PLEASURE AND PROFIT

At the beginning of the 18th century many of these estates were recorded in a series of bird's-eye views that capture the arrangement of the park and gardens as described by Defoe. In Johannes Kip's engraving of Westbury Court in Gloucestershire (left), all the necessary components for the provision of the household are shown, from vegetables and wall-trained fruit to dovecotes, fish ponds, and, to the left, a duck pond with islands adjacent to a rabbit warren. The wider estate would often be laid out as parkland containing deer and cattle.

The gardens from this period reflect the dual attributes of 'pleasure and profit', an idea well exercised by the Romans. Pliny the Younger wrote about the appeal of his country villa, with its fruit, herbs, fish ponds and vineyards, as a retreat from the busy metropolis. This was also a fundamental Renaissance principle expressed by the Roman poet Horace as *dulce et utile*, 'sweetness and use', interpreted by the 19th-century Arts and Crafts exponent William Morris in his celebrated golden rule 'have nothing in your houses that you do not know to be useful, or believe to be beautiful'.

Early self-sufficiency

The Roman occupation left a valuable legacy of horticulture and husbandry. However, it was not until the Middle Ages, when the monks laid down written codes for living, that the significance of gardens to both body and soul began to emerge.

Monastic gardens in medieval Britain supplied provisions not only for the monks but also for the local community. Acres of food were cultivated, ensuring a diet rich in vegetables, while aromatic herbs grown in the physic garden for medicinal purposes were used in the infirmary. Many healing plants, such as peonies and irises, had beautiful flowers that contributed to the ornamental appeal of the garden. Orchards, bee hives, dovecotes and a well-managed system of fish ponds were all part of both monastic and manorial establishments.

16th and 17th-century ideas

After the Reformation, the Elizabethans delighted in flowers to ornament not only their gardens but also their dining tables. Roses, borage, violets, marigolds and cowslips were candied and added to favourite desserts or distilled into perfumed water. However, it was in the 17th century that the fine balance between beauty and use was truly achieved, in equal measure, by the conflicting ideologies of the period: on the one hand the Puritans, who championed the planting of fruit trees for the common good, and on the other the Epicureans who delighted in the sensual pleasures of a ripe fruit.

Self-sufficiency was also a sign of prudent household management, as expressed in 1615 by Gervase Markham. Regarding diet, he recommends: 'let it proceed more from the provision of her [the housewife's] own yard, than the furniture of the markets', a sentiment echoed a few years later by Sir John Oglander in his *Rules of Husbandry*:

Potagers are ornamental as well as productive, as exemplified in the potager garden at Woolbeding Gardens, West Sussex, where coloured salad crops and flowers are grown together.

Provide all things unto thy house so that thou mayest not go by the penny: fish ponds, dove-house and warren, hop-garden, kitchen-garden and orchard, all sorts of poultry with convenient houses for them ... have ever a hogshead of verjuice ... if thou hast a good store of apples, make cider which, well made, is as good as white wine. Keep bees and make mead, which, with a hogshead or two of strong beer and a runlet of sack, will serve thee without French wine, which will not long be kept good.'

The ponds, deer parks and formal gardens in this 17th-century view of Charlecote Park, Warwickshire (c.1696) all provided food for the household kitchen.

USING THE LAND

Producing food contributed to the household economy by both saving money and generating income from the trade or sale of surplus goods, such as eggs, poultry and products from the beehive and dairy. This was especially important for smaller households and peasants who would have grown fruit and vegetables, kept bees and reared poultry and a pig or two in their gardens and on common land.

The country pursuits of hunting, shooting and fishing provided both sport for the family and food for the table. Deer parks offered various forms of hunting, while ponds and lakes were used for sailing, angling and, on rare occasions, entire re-enactments of celebrated naval victories.

By the early 18th century many treatises and discourses had been written on the self-sufficient estate. The Norfolk landowner Roger North wrote about gardens, buildings and fish ponds based on his own experiences, having been inspired by the 'princely econom y of the duke of Beaufort' at Badminton House in Gloucestershire where 'soap and candle were made in the house; so like-wise the malt was ground there; and all the drink, that came to the duke's table, was of malt sun-dried upon the leads of his house'. The diarist John Evelyn, North's contemporary, wrote passionately about 'roots, vegetables, herbs and fruits', but especially salads in his discourse *Acetaria* (1699). Other influential treatises included Thomas Hill's *The Profitable Art of Gardening* (1574), William Lawson's *A New Orchard and Garden* (1618) and Stephen Switzer's *The Practical Kitchen Gardener* (1727).

THE GRAND TOUR

The delicate balance between beauty and use was tipped by the 18th-century landscape revolution, producing landscapes resembling the Arcadian scenes from the classical paintings collected on the obligatory Grand Tour of Italy. Wooded hillsides, lakes and classical temples became the new style of gardening. Kitchen gardens were not part of the picture and were concealed behind shrubberies or sited away from the house, out of view.

While this new style of gardening became the latest craze in France, where it was known as 'le jardin Anglais', so no fashionable household in Britain was without a French chef, a trend that reinforced a shift in taste from sweetly fragrant flavours to appetising salt-acid sensations which formed the basis of today's British cuisine. This coincided with the improved quality of home-produced meats and a wider range of fruit and vegetables. A casualty of the new style of cooking was the diversity of herbs and spices that had defined British food since medieval times.

The translucent leaves and blood-red stems of ruby chard in the allotment gardens at Quarry Bank Mill, Cheshire.

INDUSTRIAL DEVELOPMENTS

The Industrial Revolution of the 18th and 19th centuries saw developments in glasshouse technology that transformed the cultivation of fruit. The addition of heating and irrigation systems within a revolutionary structure that did not exclude daylight extended the seasons in which crops could be produced and enabled an increasingly diverse range of exotic fruit to be grown. The kitchen garden became a status symbol and landowners competed with each other over the latest technology.

Meanwhile, the agricultural revolution improved both arable and livestock management, resulting in greater productivity and the inevitable commercialisation of farming practices necessary to feed the rapidly increasing urban population. Production became increasingly centralised as the new railway systems enabled food to be transported longer distances than before, and refrigeration and canning greatly extended the shelf-life of many products. Imports from abroad and intensive farming methods employed in the 20th century contributed to cheaper food. Consequently, there was a dramatic decline in home-produced food.

This c.1940 Dig For Victory Now poster was part of the Second World War campaign to encourage people to grow their own food during rationing, and be as self-sufficient as possible.

Your own vegetables all the year round . . . if you DIG FOR VICTORY NOW

THE COST OF WAR

With the devastation of the First World War, the work force was considerably reduced and this, together with the increased cost of living, led to the demise of most labour-intensive kitchen gardens.

However, on a smaller scale, many country-dwellers maintained a level of self-sufficiency at least until the Second World War. In an ironic twist, the valiant 'Dig for Victory' efforts of the Second World War heralded the demise of the productive garden: as a backlash against the hardship of wartime living, peacetime gardens were now to be enjoyed as an area for entertainment and relaxation. Immaculate green lawns and low-maintenance planting were the order of the day. With an increasing choice of food available in the shops, it was no longer necessary to toil in the garden.

Renewed enthusiasm

Somehow, the desire to 'grow your own' has remained deep-rooted in the nation's consciousness, re-emerging in various forms, most memorably in the 1970s television comedy *The Good Life* and, from the same decade, in John Seymour's *The Complete Book of Self-Sufficiency*, which has remained in print ever since. These provided examples of gardens that, though worthy, held no consideration for aesthetics and were diametrically opposed to their ornamental low-maintenance counterparts. However, as history proves, one element need not exclude the other – productivity and beauty can be unified in the garden.

With predicted world food shortages, local production is once again on the agenda, with high-profile exponents such as HRH the Prince of Wales growing produce in his kitchen gardens, orchards and home farm at Highgrove, his Gloucestershire estate, inspiring a new wave of self-sufficiency enthusiasts to experience the delights of growing and eating the fruits of their toil. Such has been the success of the campaign to 'grow your own' that vegetable seeds are currently outselling ornamental seeds in garden centres throughout the country.

The gardens and country estates of the past have a role to play in conveying the story to a new generation – a challenge that is being taken up by the National Trust in a variety of ways, including re-establishing kitchen gardens to provide at least a proportion of the food consumed in their cafés and restaurants, replanting orchards and leasing out land for allotment schemes. This is just the beginning of an enterprise exploring how the very same land and facilities that once supplied seasonal food to private families and households could once more be used for the good of all. For details of kitchen gardens to visit, please go to www.nationaltrust.org.uk.

Runner beans climbing up their supporting canes in the kitchen garden at Arlington Court, Devon, appreciated as much for the beauty of their scarlet flowers as for the green beans.

Fruit and Vegetables

'A good plum is certainly better than an ill peach.'

— WILLIAM TEMPLE, *Upon the Gardens of Epicurus* (1685)

Flowers, fruit and vegetables contribute to the well-ordered composition at Barrington Court, Somerset.

Growing fruit and vegetables is one aspect of self-sufficiency that can be practised by just about anyone, whether you have access to the grand walled acres of an aristocratic estate or just a tiny plot of land. Although plenty of money can be spent on elaborate structures and mature plants, most of us can grow our own produce at very little expense. Those with nothing more than a window box should not be excluded from the satisfaction of growing some favourite foods, for example a delicious salad of cherry tomatoes sprinkled with basil, or a few chilli peppers to spruce up a meal.

The story of kitchen gardening is filled with ingenuity and experimentation, much of which has been forgotten as the practice of growing crops domestically has declined. With the advantage of hindsight, we can take the best practices from the past and adapt them to our own circumstances.

Until the 18th century, flowers, fruit and vegetables were mainly grown together in the garden, most plants having some practical use. Vegetables were grown in beds, bordered by flowering plants and screened by fruit trees trained on open fences, a style later known as a polehedge. Larger establishments may have had specific kitchen gardens extending to 0.8ha (2 acres) or more to produce vegetables for the whole household, including the servants. These gardens were also referred to as 'wort gardens' or 'kale yards'. Only in the 18th century did the word 'vegetable' come to mean an edible plant.

Kitchen gardens were initially situated close to the house so that they were easily accessible. An early 18th-century view of the house and gardens at Erddig, North Wales, shows two enclosures near the house, each containing two square beds (right). A survey of these gardens from 1718 suggests that the left enclosure was known as the 'Kitchen Garden' and the right the 'Harty Choake Garden', a sign of the popularity of the artichoke at this time. The survey also lists an extensive range of wall fruit, including several varieties of peach, 'plumb', 'nectorine', 'apricock', cherry, mulberry and apple, with pears reserved for 'ye best Garden', all expertly trained as fans, espaliers or cordons (see page 48).

Book plate of Erddig, Wrexham, by Johannes Kip, in Britannia Illustrata *(1707). Walled enclosures for fruit and vegetables are shown near the house.*

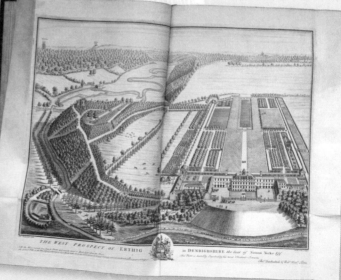

VEGETABLES

Early recipe books show that, contrary to popular belief, the British diet in all sectors of society was rich in a wide variety of vegetables eaten either as salads or stewed with meat. Beans, peas, leeks, parsnips and turnips were all grown by 1500, along with leafy vegetables such as cabbages, spinach, radishes and sorrel. Cauliflower was introduced to England just before 1600 and was initially regarded as a high-status vegetable.

Coloured woodcut (1507) showing a late medieval kitchen with a cook making pottage.

Pottage

Before the advent of sophisticated kitchens, most vegetables would have been cooked in a pot over the fire together with any meat or fish available to make a soup or stew-like dish called pottage. This was the staple diet of the majority of people in medieval England, prompting the physician Andrew Boorde, in his *Dyetary Of Helth* of 1542, to state that 'Pottage is not so much used in all Christendom as it is used in England.' Vegetables classed as 'good pottagers' included onions, leeks and colewort which, together with garlic, formed the bulk of the vegetables grown. Coleworts were a hardy type of brassica, not cut off whole like cabbage or cauliflower, but harvested as a cut-and-come-again

RECIPE

Pottage

'A good potage for dinner is thus made: Boil Beef, Mutton, Veal, Volaille [poultry], and a little piece of the Lean of a Gammon of the best Bacon, with some quartered Onions (and a little Garlick, if you like it), you need no salt, if you have Bacon, but put in a little Pepper and Cloves. If it be in the Winter, put in a Bouquet of Sweet-herbs, or whole onions, or Roots, or Cabbage. If season of Herbs, boil in a little of the broth apart, some Lettice, Sorrel, Borage, and Bugloss, &c. till they be only well mortified. If you put in any gravy, let it boil or stew a while with the broth; put it in due time upon the tosted bread to Mittoner [simmer], &c. If you boil some half rosted meat with your broth, it will be the better.'

KENELM DIGBY, *The Closet of Kenelm Digby Opened* (1669)

vegetable. Four main sowings throughout the year ensured a continual crop of young leaves.

Other vegetables that were suitable for pottage were peas and beans, both of which were field crops. These were commonly dried to preserve them before adding them to the pot, although a few beans would have been grown in gardens and eaten as fresh vegetables. The variations of pottage were endless, depending on what was available at the time.

Root vegetables

A 'pennyworth of skirret seed' represented the first garden appearance of a root crop, available initially only to the wealthy. Skirrets (*Sium sisarum*) were similar to parsnips and were parboiled and stewed in butter or rolled in flour and fried; they were said to have a sweet flavour and floury texture. Carrots were introduced in the 16th century and, as with skirrets, were eaten as individual vegetables rather than added to pottage. Carrots were 'roasted in the embers til they be tender' and eaten with vinegar and oil. The advantage of growing root vegetables was that they could be stored for use over the winter when leafy vegetables were scarce.

Over time, the once-fashionable root crops became a victim of their own high-yielding success and were relegated to the rank of staple peasant diet. In *Haven of Health* (1584) the Tudor physician Thomas Cogan described parsnips and carrots as 'common meate among common people, all the time of autumn, and chiefly upon fish daies'. Garlic, once so prolific in medieval gardens, was also losing favour, and did not fully recover until it was 'rediscovered' in the latter half of the 20th century as an essential ingredient in popular French and Italian dishes.

Carrots grown in the kitchen garden at Knightshayes Court, Devon. Carrots, once a highly esteemed root vegetable, are now a commercial staple.

Purple globe artichoke in the walled garden at Beningbrough Hall, Yorkshire. The regal artichoke was a favourite vegetable of the Tudor court.

Tudor vegetables

By the reign of Henry VIII the British diet became more varied, and the nobility in particular enjoyed the newly introduced globe artichoke (see page 18) and its relative the cardoon, both of which were also spectacular as architectural garden plants. Asparagus was another favourite, and has remained so to this day. The chronicler Ralph Holinshead noted in 1548 that 'melons, pompions [pumpkins], gourdes, cucumber, radishes, skirets, parsnips and turnips' were eaten as 'deintie dishes at the table of delicate merchants, gentlemen and the nobilitie who make their provision yearlie for new seeds out of strange countries'.

Pumpkins

Pumpkins were eaten by rich and poor alike, either simply stuffed with apples and baked, or, for a more elaborate dish, cut up and fried with herbs and spices, sugar and egg, then put in a pastry case with apple and currants to make a pumpkin pie. This was a favourite of the early colonists of North America, where it became a national dish.

Vegetables from the New World

During the 16th and 17th centuries, vegetables that had been discovered in the Americas began to take precedence in the kitchens of the wealthy households. Kidney beans, from Peru, were served boiled and buttered, and added to a salad; runner beans, which have remained a popular and easy vegetable to grow, had the added benefit of pretty scarlet flowers before offering up a prolific harvest of tasty green beans. However, by far the most significant vegetable to make its way over from America was the potato, first introduced in the 1560s by Admiral Sir John Hawkins. He discovered it on 'the coast of Guinea and the Indies of Nova Hispania' but it is thought that this was not the common potato but sweet potato (*Ipomea batata*),

KITCHEN GARDEN ESTATE

described by the Elizabethan traveller Richard Hakluyt in his *Discourse on Western Planting* (1584) as 'the most delicate rootes that may be eaten, and doe farre exceed our passeneps or carrots ... more delicious than any sweet apple sugred'. The common white potato (*Solanum tuberosum*) did not reach Britain until the very end of the 16th century.

Initially potatoes were used as a filling for tarts. An early recipe from 1596 combined potatoes with borage roots, quinces, dates, egg yolks, wine, sugar, spices and 'the brains of 3 or 4 cock sparrows'. They did not become the universal staple that they are today for another two hundred years, when they were heralded as suitable food for both rich and poor, especially good when roasted with meat, and the ultimate luxury when mashed to a soft, creamy texture. Their economic value, according to the Victorian housewife's champion Mrs Beeton, lay in the fact that an acre of potatoes would feed double the number of people that could be fed from an acre of wheat.

A 16th-century coloured engraving of Sir John Hawkins (1532–95), Elizabethan adventurer, slave trader, spy and naval commander, who introduced the sweet potato to Britain.

The Mediterranean influence

The heritage of British food is the result of a happy blend of native ingredients and exciting influences from foreign travel and trade links. One of the most notable commentators on our food was Giacomo Castelvetro, an Italian who, on moving to England in the early 17th century, was dismayed at the way we cooked our fruit and vegetables. He decided to remedy this by writing *A Brief Account of the Fruit, Herbs and Vegetables of Italy* (1614), dedicated to his patron, Lucy, Countess of Bedford. The book described Italian methods of preparing food and nearly a century later the diarist John Evelyn, returning from his travels to Italy, advocated the same light touch of the Italian cuisine. However, it would not be for another 250 years that the flavours of southern Europe were brought back to our attention by the influential cookery writer Elizabeth David in her book *Mediterranean Food* (1950).

The beauty of Castelvetro's recipes is in their very simplicity, ideal for today's busy lifestyles. Although we may frown upon the quantity of butter it was nearly always counteracted by the use of vinegar, wine or verjuice. Similar to cider or a mild vinegar, verjuice was made in Britain from crab apples and in Italy from unripe grapes. It was used extensively in cooking (see page 76).

GLOBE ARTICHOKE

A hardy perennial native to southern Europe, globe artichoke (*Cynara scolymus*) was a familiar vegetable to the Ancient Greeks and Romans. It was introduced to Britain in the 16th century and, as a favourite food of Henry VIII, was soon heralded as a high-status vegetable. According to Castelvetro it is best to 'Select some small ones and cut off the tips of the pointed outer leaves, boil them first in fresh water to take away the bitterness, and then finish cooking them in rich beef or chicken broth. Serve them in a shallow dish on slices of bread moistened with just a little of the broth, sprinkled with grated mature cheese and pepper to bring out their goodness.'

BROAD BEANS

These were one of the earliest varieties of bean to be cultivated in Britain, long before the New World introductions of the Elizabethan period. Castelvetro says the Italians eat the young broad beans (*Vicia fava*) raw at the end of a meal with a salty cheese or parmesan, and always with pepper; if there is no cheese, they can just be eaten with salt. When the beans become big, boil them in water and remove the tough skin, then 'put the beans in a little pot with oil or fresh butter, and sweet herbs chopped very fine, add salt and pepper and stew gently, to make a really tasty little dish'.

CUCUMBER

Cucumbers (*Cucumis sativus*) were cultivated by the Ancient Romans in frames of hot dung, a tradition that continued in kitchen gardens around Britain throughout the centuries. Although they are usually considered a salad vegetable, Castelvetro recommends serving cucumbers as a hot stuffed dish by cutting them in half lengthways and hollowing out the soft part inside. 'Then fill them with a stuffing of finely chopped herbs, breadcrumbs, an egg, grated cheese and oil or butter, all mixed together. Roast them on a grid, or cook them gently in an earthenware pot ... you could add pepper or spices.'

FIELD MUSHROOMS

While not strictly a vegetable, mushrooms were an important part of the Italian diet and would originally have been gathered from the wild; it was only in the middle of the 17th century that gardeners in France began to experiment with their cultivation. Mushroom houses were a feature of the Victorian kitchen garden (see page 43) and mushrooms a favourite at the dinner table. Italian cuisine in particular makes good use of a wide range of mushrooms. Castelvetro suggests cooking field mushrooms (*Agaricus campestris*) gently with a little water, plenty of oil or butter, garlic, salt, pepper and a 'decent amount of sweet herbs. Serve them sprinkled with bitter orange juice, or a little verjuice'. He goes on to challenge the reader that 'Whoever eats them like this and doesn't lick their fingers doe not, in my opinion, know much about true gluttony.'

SPINACH

Long cultivated in Britain, spinach (*Spinacia oleracea*) was considered by Castelvetro to be a 'good and wholesome garden plant', to be eaten either on its own or with other vegetables and herbs such as beets, parsley and borage. Traditionally, it was cooked briefly in salted water and served with oil, pepper, a little verjuice and raisins. Alternatively, once boiled, it can be chopped very finely and 'finished cooking on a low heat in a pan with oil or butter, seasoned with salt and pepper with raisins mixed in'. According to Castelvetro, 'this makes a really delicious dish' often used as a filling for tarts, or *tortelli* which are fried in oil or butter and served with honey 'or better still, sugar'.

Salads

As fresh leafy vegetables increased in popularity in the 17th century, so pottage went out of fashion. Early salads were composed of an exciting variety of lettuces, herb leaves, vegetables, pickles, nuts and fruit, enjoyed not only during the summer months but also in winter when boiled salads were served. These consisted of vegetables cooked in butter and seasoned with spices, sugar and vinegar, or verjuice. By the 19th century the components of a salad were simplified in favour of a combination of lettuce and cress, cucumber, radishes, beetroot, celery and spring onions, dressed with salt, pepper, vinegar, mustard and oil, much as we would make it today (see pages 64–66).

Spinach, considered a 'good and wholesome garden plant' by Castelvetro in the early 17th century, growing in the kitchen garden at Knightshayes Court, Devon.

Vegetables in the Georgian period

During the 18th century a wide variety of vegetables continued to be grown in the kitchen gardens of country-house estates. Contemporary accounts from Kingston Lacy in Dorset record a selection that includes spinach, turnips, parsnips, sprouts, cabbage, artichokes, carrots, peas and asparagus. Salsify (*Tragopogon porrifolius*) was a highly esteemed root vegetable which eventually fell from favour but is increasingly found on restaurant menus today. Commonly known as the 'vegetable oyster' because of its subtle fish flavour, it had been cultivated in France since the 1700s and would have been used by the wave of French chefs employed in the most fashionable British households at the time. It is a tall, handsome plant equally attractive in the ornamental garden if it is allowed to flower. Scorzonera (*Scorzonera hispanica*) is similar to salsify but with a black skin. John Evelyn was familiar with this vegetable and claimed 'a more excellent root there is hardly growing'.

Polite Georgian society would have enjoyed green leafy vegetables, peas and beans served with copious amounts of melted butter. As the use of spices declined, British food was gaining a reputation for blandness. Charles Moritz, a Swiss traveller, wrote disparagingly in 1782 that the ordinary Englishman's midday meal usually consisted of 'a piece of half boiled or half roasted meat; a few cabbage leaves, boiled in plain water; on which they pour a sauce made of flour and butter, the usual method of dressing vegetables in England'. Old favourites such as artichokes and asparagus remained a speciality, rather than commonplace, despite the ease with which they could be cultivated.

The salsify flower is equally attractive in the kitchen or ornamental garden.

RECIPE

Salsify Recipe

Peel then boil or steam the roots, tied together in bundles, until they are tender. Cut loose and fry until golden brown. Alternatively, dip in egg and coat in breadcrumbs before frying for an extra crunchy coating, and serve with a slice of lemon to mimic a superior version of a fish finger.

SEA KALE

One native vegetable that caught the attention of another traveller in the 18th century was sea kale (*Crambe maritima*), a member of the asparagus family which the Finnish botanist Per Kalm described as 'one of the best flavoured green vegetables which anyone can wish for'. The Victorians considered it the aristocrat of the kitchen garden where it was widely grown, being easily digestible and nutritious.

Sea kale is one of the few vegetables that needs to be forced in the dark before harvesting. Root cuttings, called thongs, are planted in mid-March and grown on for a year. The following year the plants are covered with a sea kale forcer or upturned bucket until the blanched shoots are ready for harvesting by mid-April. The plant will produce leaves year after year. They are eaten steamed and served with butter.

The 19th century

In Victorian Britain, wealthy households created large kitchen gardens to grow ever-increasing varieties of vegetables. Supplying the household with produce out of season was the ultimate challenge. Artichoke and cauliflower remained in high esteem in all the grand houses and the increasingly popular potatoes were served sometimes three times a day, prepared in a different way each time. By now the medieval staples of onions, leeks and garlic had fallen out of fashion, for the most part only used to flavour soups and stocks. Garlic was unpopular in middle-class households but was occasionally consumed in more cosmopolitan sections of society. The tomato, technically a fruit, was originally introduced from the New World as an ornamental plant in the 16th century but only became popular as a salad ingredient towards the end of the 19th.

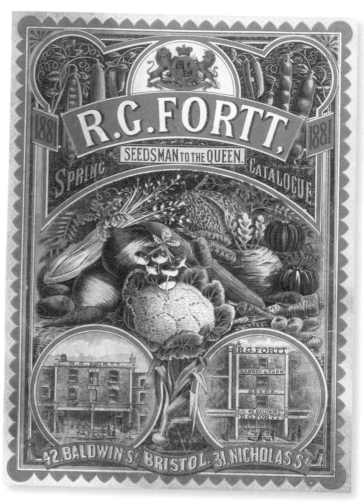

R. G. Fortt's spring gardening catalogue (1881). Catalogues like these met the Victorian demand for ever-increasing varieties of vegetables.

Fruit

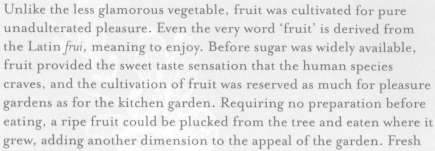

Unlike the less glamorous vegetable, fruit was cultivated for pure unadulterated pleasure. Even the very word 'fruit' is derived from the Latin *frui*, meaning to enjoy. Before sugar was widely available, fruit provided the sweet taste sensation that the human species craves, and the cultivation of fruit was reserved as much for pleasure gardens as for the kitchen garden. Requiring no preparation before eating, a ripe fruit could be plucked from the tree and eaten where it grew, adding another dimension to the appeal of the garden. Fresh fruit was part of the dessert course, but fruit was also candied, made into ices, fools and jellies, and cooked with savoury dishes, especially game. Preserved as sweetmeats, jams and cordials, fruit could be enjoyed well into the winter months. From the 18th century, the wealthy began to spend the 'season' in London, so fruit and other produce would be sent to their town address, carefully packaged to ensure they arrived in perfect condition.

Plums growing in the orchard at Lyveden New Bield, Northamptonshire. The recently restored garden contains an orchard of the sort of fruit varieties that would have been available in Elizabethan times.

Exotic fruit were introduced via the early trade links with southern Europe, in particular citrus fruit. The Elizabethans enjoyed candied slices of lemon and Sir Hugh Platt, in his *Delights for Ladies* (1605), gives instructions for keeping orange juice all year round to make sauces and drinks. Oranges earned their place in the heritage of British cuisine as marmalade. The name derived from a Portuguese quince paste, but was adopted by the British for the preserve made from the bitter Seville orange.

During the 16th and 17th centuries the taste for foreign imports, together with advanced gardening techniques, encouraged people to try to grow their own exotic fruit such as figs apricots and peaches in their gardens at home, making use of south-facing walls for extra warmth and protection.

In his *Five Hundreth Pointes of Good Husbandrie* (1557), Thomas Tusser lists 27 different fruit trees and bushes, including the newly introduced fruit such as apricots and melons, along with medieval favourites such as apples of differing varieties, pears, plums, damsons, bullaces, cherries and the three medieval stalwarts medlars, mulberries and quinces. Also listed are grapes, bilberries, strawberries (which would have been the small but flavoursome wild variety) and gooseberries, once the height of fashion.

A much wider variety of fruit seems to have been grown than today: by 1629, in his *Paradisi in Sole*, the botanist John Parkinson lists for example 57 varieties of apples, 62 pears, 61 plums, 35 cherries and 22 peaches.

By the early 18th century Batty Langley produced a comprehensive plan of a fruit garden (below) in his *New Principles of Gardening* (1728). It comprises 262 trees altogether, with a predominance of pears planted as espaliers and grouped according to their season, followed by cherries, apples and peaches, plus quantities of nectarines, apricots, figs, grapes, plums, codlins (a small apple used for cooking) and four mulberry trees. The plan is so well annotated it could be used as a base plan today.

Mezzotint print of the early 18th-century garden designer Batty Langley, by J. Carwitham (1741).

Batty Langley's plan of a fruit garden from his book New Principles of Gardening *(1728).*

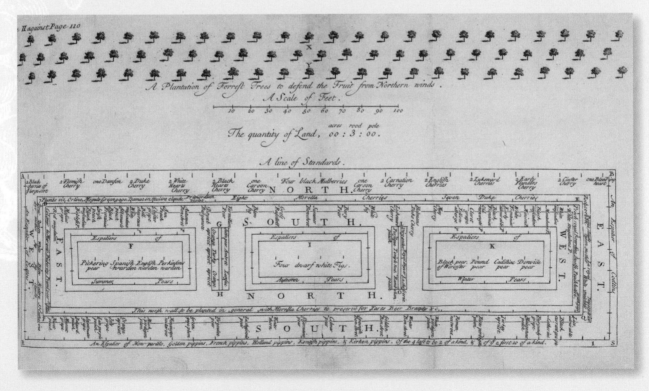

Gooseberries

This most typical of British fruit has an illustrious history, first recorded in Britain in 1275 when they were ordered from France to be planted at the Tower of London. By the 16th century gooseberries were widely grown, used to fill tarts and for sauces, as well as for making wine. Most would have been too sharp to eat raw, but on a visit to Woburn in Bedfordshire in 1697 the intrepid 17th-century traveller Celia Fiennes noted in her diary that she ate 'a great quantity of the Red Carolina goosbery which is a large thin skin'd sweete goosbery', confirming the introduction of dessert varieties. During the 18th and 19th centuries gooseberries were adopted by the many weaving communities in the North of England as a fruit to exhibit at local annual shows. Because of a tax imposed on sugar, an essential ingredient for sweetening the sharp-flavoured fruit and for jam-making, gooseberries were not commercially cultivated until 1876 when the tax was repealed.

Gooseberries are well suited to the British climate and are included in some of the most typical British dishes, such as

Gooseberries are well suited to the British climate and were highly esteemed for their versatility.

RECIPE

Gooseberries in Honey Saffron Cream

SERVES 6
225g (8oz) gooseberries
50g (2oz) caster sugar
6 egg yolks
600ml (1 pint) single
  cream
75g (3oz) honey
¼ tsp saffron

Preheat the oven to 140°C (275°F, Gas Mark 1). Put the gooseberries into a pan with the sugar and 2 tablespoons of cold water. Cover tightly and stew gently for 5 minutes until tender. Divide between 6 ramekins.

Whisk the egg yolks with the cream, honey and saffron and pour into a bowl set over simmering water. Cook the custard gently, stirring regularly for 10 minutes until it coats the back of a spoon. Strain it over the gooseberries.

Stand the ramekins in a bain-marie of warm water and bake in the oven until set. Serve warm or cold.

crumbles and fools. The flavour of gooseberries marries very well with elderflower, happily available at the same time of year. The sharper varieties complement savoury dishes, especially oily fish such as mackerel. When trained as small standard bushes they are ideal ornaments to the kitchen garden.

Red and white currants

The berries of red and white currants are among the most beautiful fruit in the garden, especially when trained against a wall like a beaded curtain. The redcurrant is closely related to the blackcurrant, while the whitecurrant is an albino form of the red. Currants have been grown in British gardens since the 16th century, originally called 'raisins of Corinth', supposedly for resembling the dried grapes that were imported from Greece. In the early 17th century John Tradescant introduced a large improved variety of redcurrant from Holland called the 'Great Red', along with many other valuable plants destined for the celebrated gardens at Hatfield House in Hertfordshire. This association, along with its improved flavour, secured the redcurrant's position as one of the nation's most highly esteemed fruits, surpassed only by the newly developed modern strawberry two hundred years later. Like gooseberries, currants would have been grown in the most ornamental areas of the garden, as standards and bushes or trained on a wall. One advantage the pearl-like whitecurrant has over the red is that it is less attractive to birds.

The redcurrant has been celebrated in Britain since the 16th century for its flavour and ornamental properties.

Strawberries

Strawberries are believed to be named either from their habit of 'straying' as they throw out new little plants, or from the practice of laying straw underneath the fruit to protect it from the damp ground. The present garden and commercially grown strawberry was unknown in Britain until the 19th century. Prior to that the small wild strawberry was cossetted by gardeners to ensure it grew plump and juicy. Even as a small fruit it was much loved, enjoyed on its own or with a dollop of cream.

Strawberries, the fruit synonymous with British summer, fresh from the garden.

Strawberry and Verjuice Custard Tart

This tart recaptures the old traditions of steeping fruit in verjuice.

SERVES 6–8
450g (1lb) strawberries
115g (4oz) caster sugar
4 tsp verjuice (or 2 tsp
  cider vinegar and 2
  tsp lemon juice)
225g (8oz) sweet
  shortcrust pastry
60g (2oz) plain flour
30g (1oz) golden
  caster sugar
grated zest of ½ lemon
1 egg, plus 2 egg yolks
450ml (15fl oz)
  single cream

TO SERVE
lemon juice
caster sugar
double cream

Before you start, preheat the oven to 190°C (375°F, Gas Mark 5). Hull three-quarters of the strawberries, then cut them into halves or quarters. Place them in a bowl and stir in half the caster sugar. Add the verjuice, stir well, then set aside for 30 minutes.

Line a deep 23cm (9in) tart tin with the pastry, then line the pastry with greaseproof paper or kitchen foil and cover with dried beans or rice to prevent the pastry from rising. Bake in the oven for about 10 minutes until the pastry case is lightly coloured. Remove from the oven, take out the lining and beans or rice, then return to the oven for 3–4 minutes.

Mix the flour, golden caster sugar and lemon zest in a bowl and then sprinkle over the pastry base. Drain the strawberry mixture well, reserving the fruit and juice separately, then place the strawberries in the pastry case.

Make the egg custard by whisking the eggs, egg yolks and remaining caster sugar in a bowl. Heat the cream in a pan until almost boiling, then gradually add the cream to the egg and sugar mixture, stirring. Add some of the juice from the strawberries (depending how much there is) and stir to mix. Pour over the strawberries in the pastry case so that some strawberries are just poking through the surface of the custard.

Bake in the oven for about 35–40 minutes or until just set, well risen and golden brown. Remove from the oven and allow to cool to room temperature. While the tart cools, slice the remaining strawberries, add some lemon juice and sugar and stir to mix. Leave to macerate for a few minutes, then serve the tart with the sliced strawberries and some cream.

Training and grafting in the 17th century

The geometric gardens of the 16th and 17th centuries reflected an overriding desire to control nature. Fruit trees were ideally suited to grafting and pruning techniques which were exploited whenever possible. Texts from the Italian Renaissance made their way over to the libraries of the British nobility. One such influential book was Giambattista Della Porta's *Magia Naturalis*, originally published in 1558 and translated into English a century later. Della Porta explains how to manipulate nature so that you can have fruit and flowers 'at all times of the year', and how to grow extra-large fruit, or fruit without a stone or kernel. He also describes how to make fruits and flowers 'be of diverse colours, such as are not naturally incident to their kind' and to grow fruit to resemble 'all figures and impressions whatever'. To outwit nature by grafting one fruit upon another was the greatest challenge, the results seemingly close to magic: 'and not only every tree can be grafted onto every tree, but one tree may be adulterated with them all'. In *The English Husbandman* (1613), Gervase Markham advocated grafting to develop new kinds of fruit:

Woodcut from Giambattista Della Porta's Magia Naturalis *(1558), which explains how to 'manipulate nature' using grafting techniques.*

Effects, wonders and strange issues which do proceede from many quaint motions and helps in grafting, as thus: if you will have Peaches, Cherryes, Quinces, Medlars, Damson, or any Plumbe whatsoever to ripen early ... you shall then graft them onto Mulberrystocke; ... if you graft Apples, Peares or any fruit upon a Figge-tree stock, they will bear fruit without blooming; if you take an apple graft, a pear graft of like biggnesse, and having cloven them, join them as one body in grafting, the fruit they bring forth will be halfe Apple and halfe Peare, and so likewise of all other fruits which are of contrary tastes and natures.

These seemingly advanced techniques had been practised since at least the Roman period, recurring many times throughout the history of English gardening. The Victorians enjoyed experimenting still further and today grafting techniques have produced 'family' trees which each bear several different fruit, aimed at small gardens where there may be room for only a single tree.

Grafting caused an inevitable backlash from the Puritan elements of the population, who preferred a less adulterated version of nature as expressed by the 17th-century poet Andrew Marvell in 'The Mower against Gardens':

Had he not dealt between the bark and tree,

Forbidden mixtures there to see.

No plant now knew the stock from which it came;

He grafts upon the wild the tame:

That uncertain and adulterous fruit

Might put the palate in dispute.

Pears respond well to training, making attractive architectural features in the garden, as at Bateman's, East Sussex.

Sir William Temple and the Epicureans

After the English Civil War and the sackcloth lifestyle of the Puritan-led republic, the joys of fruit were once again embraced in Restoration Britain and a truce was drawn between the opposing camps: the Puritan perception of the virtuous benefits of fruit and the sensuous pleasures enjoyed by the Epicureans. No one delighted more in fruit than Sir William Temple, the British Ambassador to the Hague, whose passion is captured in his essay *Upon the Gardens of Epicurus* (1685). We learn from Temple that 'no country equals us in the variety of fruits which may be justly called good; and from the

The Epicurean's delight: A still life of voluptuous fruit by Joris van Son (1623–1667), depicting grapes, quince, medlar, cherries and strawberries.

earliest cherry and strawberry to the last apples and pears, may furnish every day of the circling year', boasting further that 'Italians have agreed, my white figs are to be as good as any of that sort in Italy'. The notoriously damp British climate does indeed lend itself to growing a diverse range of fruit for a large part of the year, something which should make its inhabitants justly proud and which should be exploited further.

A rare surviving late 17th-century garden at Westbury Court in Gloucestershire, where fruit trees and vegetables grow side by side with ornamentals, evokes the gardens that Temple so delighted in. The garden has been restored by the National Trust using, where possible, pre-1700 varieties of fruit. In gardens of this period, barely a wall would have been left unfurnished with fan-trained fruit trees, as identified in the many bird's-eye views of the country estates recorded by Kip and Knyff in *Britannia Illustrata* (1707), (see page 6), and in an evocative painting by John Griffier the Elder of Sudbury Hall in Derbyshire, which shows every wall supporting fan-trained fruit bushes underplanted with flowers and standard trees in the formal compartments, of which several would have been fruit trees (right). These images are supported by contemporary accounts, such as the journal of Celia Fiennes. On visiting Coleshill in Wiltshire in the late 17th century, she commented on the dwarf standard trees, grown among flowering varieties in the formal gardens, 'many steps and tarresses and gravel walkes with all sorts of dwarfe trees, fruit trees with standing apricock and flower trees, abundance of garden roome and filled with all sorts of things improved for pleasure and use'.

The art of dwarfing fruit trees had developed on the Continent. The techniques were introduced to Britain when the Protestant Huguenot population fled oppression in France to settle here, bringing their advanced horticultural skills with them. Dwarfing was achieved by grafting a fruit tree on to a slow-growing rootstock, and was especially useful to contain the size of cherries, naturally very large trees, for use in the formal gardens. This method is still widely employed in the nursery trade today.

The rise of the landscape park

The dramatic revolution in landscape design that swept the country in the mid-18th century put a nail in the coffin of the expansive formal gardens and their walled compartments in favour of the naturalistic English landscape park. These new Arcadian landscapes were inspired by idealised images of Ancient Greece and Rome, where there was little place for utility. Along with all the service quarters, the kitchen gardens were concealed from view. Because of its long associations with classical mythology, some fruit continued to be grown in the ornamental pleasure grounds, trained as 'fruit-hedges', or as swags of vines and passionfruit between the trees. Specific fruit gardens were planted with an 'upper' crop, such as apples, pears, cherries, plums and walnuts, beneath which was planted a 'lower' crop of raspberries, gooseberries, currants and strawberries, a method advocated by the exponents of forest gardening today (see page 50). However, most fruit for the table was by now cultivated in the new walled kitchen gardens built specifically to provide all the food necessary for the household.

Sudbury Hall from the South by John Griffier the Elder (c.1690). The garden walls at Sudbury Hall, Derbyshire, are shown clothed in trained fruit trees.

WALLED KITCHEN GARDENS

Although 18th- and 19th-century kitchen gardens were built out of sight, they were certainly not intended to be out of mind. They were expensive to construct and would have employed all the latest technological advances to produce a maximum crop over the longest possible period. As such they were very much status symbols, and would have been flaunted to visitors and friends taking a tour of the estate grounds.

In the 18th century, the walls were often heated by a furnace system of horizontal flues and supported glass lean-tos to encourage early fruiting of peaches and apricots. Fresh dung and tanners' bark (fermenting oak bark, a waste product from the leather-tanning industry) were essential for raising prestigious fruit such as melons and pineapples, and bell jars and cloches provided protection for early produce. The layout of the kitchen garden consisted of four main beds, or 'quarters', separated by rolled paths and planted in rotation with brassicas, legumes, onions and root crops. Borders along the walls were mainly planted with fruit trees and bushes, espaliered against the wall to benefit from the additional heat of the brick and underplanted with salad crops or flowers. Perennial vegetables such as globe artichokes and asparagus had their own separate borders. Some gardens contained a mushroom house, as well as a dipping pond, usually featured in the centre of the garden, for essential irrigation during dry spells.

By the 19th century, vast glasshouse structures were being created, using newly developed engineering techniques to grow exotic fruit and flowers that their owners were proud to show off to visitors.

After the First World War the expense of maintaining kitchen gardens became prohibitive and many were grassed over or fell into disrepair, but a renewed appreciation of the horticultural value of these walled gardens, together with the current interest in growing fruit and vegetables, has resulted in the restoration of several surviving examples, such as Holkham Hall in Norfolk, Kingston Lacy in Dorset, Tatton Park in Cheshire and, most famously, Heligan in Cornwall.

Layout and paths

Kitchen gardens were often sited near the stables for easy access to the manure – the ideal fertiliser and soil conditioner. The orientation of walled kitchen gardens was usually south-west to make the most of the evening sun and retain as much of the heat as possible throughout the night. They were usually square or rectangular in plan and divided into quarters edged with low box hedges and espaliered fruit trees, which defined the separate boundaries and screened the borders while contributing to the aesthetic appeal of the garden. The paths were mainly made of gravel as it was hard-wearing, comfortable to walk on and reflected heat on to the walls. Grass paths possessed none of these qualities and were not considered suitable as they would suffer from wear and tear.

Walls

As well as security and shelter, walls provided a warm surface ideally suited to training fruit. They varied in height, depending on their use and orientation. The south-facing wall was usually the highest, sometimes up to 5.5–6m (18–20ft) high in very large gardens. It protected the garden from the cold north wind and provided enough height for the glasshouses that were built against it. The east and west walls might be lower, up to 4.2m (14ft) high, with the north-facing wall only up to 3–3.6m (10–12ft) high so as to minimise the shadows it would cast on the garden. Sometimes it was done away with altogether. Some kitchen gardens had more than four walls: Humphrey Repton built several six- or seven-sided kitchen gardens in the 1790s with hexagonal dairies and fruit houses to match.

The warm brick walls of the kitchen garden at Llanerchaeron, part of a c.18th-century estate near Aberaeron, Ceredigion. The fruit tree in the centre still shows evidence of its formative training as an espalier.

Brick was the most common material for building kitchen-garden walls, providing a strong, dry and heat-retaining surface. Nails for fruit supports could easily be knocked into the lime mortar between the bricks. Over the years the walls became pitted with thousands of tiny holes from such nails, which are still in evidence today, and occasionally the walls are embedded with an old nail or plant label, a reminder of their past use.

Due to the high price of brick, the wall was one of the greatest expenses of the kitchen garden. In some instances the outer wall was faced with local stone to match the house and blend in with the landscape. Walls that were constructed entirely of stone were more durable than brick but lacked the warmth, and they needed to be close-jointed to avoid harbouring insects in the crevices. A cheaper alternative material was cob, which required copings of thatch or tiles to deter rain damage. These walls can be remarkably durable if properly maintained and surviving examples can be found, particularly in south-west England. A rare, 19th-century, crinkle-crankle example still survives at The Sanctuary in Devon (left).

A rare example of a 19th-century, crinkle-crankle wall constructed in cob, at The Sanctuary, Devon.

Occasionally walls were serpentine or zigzagged to maximise the surface area of the wall while providing protective alcoves for the fruit. These 'crinkle-crankle' walls, as they were sometimes called, were stronger than straight walls so needed to be only half as thick, therefore economising on expensive brick. The majority of these walls were built between 1796 and 1814, just after the introduction of the Brick Tax in 1784. A popular theory was that they were built by Napoleonic prisoners of war, suggesting they were of French design, yet no walls of this construction have been found in France although they are commonly found in the Netherlands. Several exist today, many in East Anglia, the longest example at Easton Hall in Suffolk.

The orientation of the walls dictated what was planted against them. Those facing south were reserved for apricots, peaches and nectarines, which require the warmest site. Acid fruits such as gooseberries, currants, morello cherries and mulberries, along

KITCHEN GARDEN ESTATE

with late varieties of plums and pears, could be planted on the north-facing walls. Sweet cherries, early plum, apples and figs faced east, while peaches, greengages and early pears thrived facing west.

The borders beneath the walls were planted with shallow-rooting crops that would not compete for nutrients with the fruit trees. South-facing borders grew aromatic herbs, early lettuces and peas, early and late kidney beans, early broad beans and strawberries. Flowers for cutting were cultivated in the west- and east-facing borders, while the north-facing border was used for growing on seedlings in spring.

Ripening peaches benefiting from the warmth of a west-facing brick wall at Barrington Court, Somerset.

Artificial heating

The advantage of heating a wall had long been recognised. As early as 1608, Sir Hugh Platt mentions fruit walls with sun-trapping niches and alcoves. He also suggested growing fruit on the walls warmed by the kitchen chimney. As the son of a brewer Platt was familiar with boilers and furnaces, but another 100 years would pass before walls were constructed specifically for the benefit of growing plants. In the early 18th century a sloping wall, at an angle of 45 degrees, was built at Belvoir Castle in Leicestershire to grow vines, with small stoves installed behind the walls and the hot air carried by flues. However, heat distribution was erratic and it was not until the 1820s that most of the associated problems with the heated wall system were ironed out by the introduction of hot-water pipes. Both systems continued to be used until the late 19th century but hot walls eventually lost favour; the risk of burning young shoots was ever-present so they were only fired up in the summer to ripen fruit. The early spring blossom was now protected by glass screens or canvas fixed to the walls in a variety of ways.

Evidence of hot walls is indicated by small archways low down and often in pairs, on the outside of a south-facing wall with flues to allow the heat to flow throughout the wall. A hot wall was also wider than other walls in the kitchen garden, being 60cm (2ft) thick from front to back.

FRUIT AND VEGETABLES

Beds

The kitchen garden was designed to have a number of separate beds to facilitate a system of crop rotation. This was essential as crops have specific soil and mineral requirements and those that share the same needs were grouped together.

'Hotbeds' had been used for centuries in Spain and the Middle East but directions were first given in England in 1577 by Thomas Hill, who explained how to protect young plants with light straw mattresses or wooden boards that could be lifted on or off. He did not use the term 'hotbed'; Parkinson appears to have been the first to do so in 1629. Hotbeds worked on the principle of fermenting matter such as compost, manure and especially tanners' bark generating heat which was used to force fruit and vegetables. Melons and cucumbers were two of the particular favourites. The steaming manure or compost was formed into raised beds, slightly sloping towards the sun, covered in 30cm (12in) or more of soil and left to ferment, protected from the weather by matting, straw or any other suitable material and set within a glass-lidded frame. Because of the unsightly appearance of hotbeds, they were generally grouped together in a separate enclosure known as the 'melonry' or 'frameyard'.

At Trengwainton in Cornwall, a rare example of raised sloping beds built in the 1820s was designed for maximum production of fruit and vegetables (left). Not only did the design increase the surface area available, it also maximised the beneficial rays of the winter sun.

Lettuces growing in the kitchen garden at Trengwainton, Cornwall. The early 19th-century kitchen garden was created with raised sloping beds to maximise exposure to the sun.

Irrigation

Water was carried in carts and barrows from nearby rivers, lakes or reservoirs, or from water towers, pumps, tanks, dipping pools and wells. Initially it would have been extracted by water wheels, but by the 19th century hydraulic ram-pumps were used. A system of water-fed alleys was designed to irrigate whole beds, whereas a watering can would be used for individual plants where necessary.

Glasshouses

It was the technical innovations of the Industrial Revolution leading to the improved design of glasshouses that had the greatest impact on fruit growing, culminating in the Victorian excesses. Exotic fruit, previously only available when imported, could now be grown at home all year round, and wealthy families who were able to afford the luxury of these glass creations competed with each other to produce the most exotic fruit for the dinner table.

At Sawbridgeworth, Hertfordshire, in the mid-19th century, the fruit grower Thomas Rivers cultivated oranges, pomegranates, lychees, guavas, mangos and even bananas, while at Cragside in Northumberland during the late 19th century, Sir William Armstrong devised a way of growing fruit trees in his glasshouses by using turntables on which the pots could be rotated (above), ensuring equal distribution of sunlight to each plant. He also devised a system, based on railway tracks, that enabled the plants to be moved outside, as described in *The Garden* magazine (1872):

The glass erections, which are of considerable extent, are devoted principally to the cultivation of fruit trees in pots. The engineering skill possessed by Sir William has enabled him to introduce a somewhat novel mode of treating trees in pots. In one house, the floor, which is of timber, is made to rest upon wheels, exactly like a railway truck; these wheels are placed upon rails which extend sufficiently far beyond the house to allow the platform with its load to run clear out into the open air, the end of the house being so constructed as to permit this to be done. By means of the turn of a handle the whole is set in motion, and finally stands still of its own accord where it is wanted, while by reversing the handle the platform with its load moves back again to its place in the house. All this is accomplished by hydraulic pressure.

Three fruits were to be the major influence on the evolution of the glasshouse: the orange, the pineapple and the grape.

The orchard house display at Cragside, Northumberland, complete with its quirky system of turntables for rotating pots to promote balanced growth.

THE ORANGERY

Oranges were a much-coveted fruit in Britain from the 16th century, when the bitter Seville orange was introduced from Spain. Lord Burghley and Sir Francis Carew of Beddington in Surrey are thought to have been the first to grow them in this country; Carew bought his trees in France in 1562. Although the plants were too tender for the cold British climate the trees would have been planted in the open ground, with winter shelter being provided by, according to the diarist John Evelyn, a 'tabernackle of boards warmed by means of stoves'. Evelyn loved citrus fruit and was pivotal in the evolution of greenhouse technology. The terms 'greenhouse' and 'orangery' were interchangeable at this time, 'greens' being the term for evergreen plants that were generally considered tender.

Bitter rather than sweet oranges were the first to be grown in most northern countries, the fruit being turned into sauces for meat, and the rind candied or dried and made into a powder for flavouring. Seedling oranges, when grown on a hotbed, were picked when about 2.5cm (1in) high and put into salads, giving them a 'marvellous fine aromaticke or spicy taste, very acceptable', according to John Parkinson in his *Paradisi in Sole Paradisus Terrestris* (1629). Besides citrus, other evergreens grown in the orangery were bay trees, myrtles and oleanders.

'The orangery' also referred to the area of the garden in which orange trees were displayed in the summer months. Traditionally, pots were placed in a sheltered position in the most formal areas of the garden, either integrated within a parterre or along a terrace or a wall. In 1698 Celia Fiennes visited Bretby in Derbyshire, where she saw the citrus displayed in the gardens: 'beyond … is a row of orange and lemon trees set in the ground, of a man's height and pretty big, full of flowers and some large fruit almost ripe; this has a penthouse over it which is cover'd up very close in the winter; … this leads to a great wilderness and just by it is another square with a fountaine whose brim is deck'd with flower potts full of flowers and all sorts of greens, on either side are 2 or 3 rows of orange and lemon trees in boxes one below another in growth.'

This describes both a permanent display with winter protection and a temporary tiered display, pre-empting Lord Burlington's Orange Tree Garden at Chiswick House in London, the flagship of the new style that was evolving in the 18th century. The garden was

Detail from a portrait attributed to Michael Dahl (c.1659–1743) of Sarah Lascelles with an orange tree. The representation of an orange in a society portrait reinforces the status of the fruit at this time. As oranges can take up to a year to ripen, the trees have the unusual habit, shown here, of flowering and fruiting at the same time.

designed by William Kent as an Italianate amphitheatre of turf steps, furnished with containerised orange trees in the summer.

Once the orangeries were emptied of their pots in the summer months, they would be used for alternative displays such as sculpture or maps, and would be transformed into a suitable room for entertaining, drinking tea, playing cards or quiet relaxation away from the house.

Orangeries made use of the latest technical innovations, employing hot-water pipes for heating and maximising the sun's energy. They were the forerunners of the magnificent glasshouses designed by Joseph Paxton and his contemporaries in the 19th century. The earliest surviving orangery in Britain, dating from the 1670s, is at Ham House in London. Like the main house, it is built of brick and is relatively plain in design. By the 18th century the orangery had developed into an often classical-style building with long south-facing windows and a solid opaque roof, and was itself an architectural feature situated either within the kitchen garden or adjacent to the house. Alternatively, the classically designed buildings were ideal eyecatchers within the landscape park, such as Robert Adam's Temple Greenhouse at Croome Park in Worcestershire (below), which had an underfloor heating system.

One of the most exceptional examples of a classically designed orangery is Robert Adam's Temple Greenhouse at Croome Park, Worcestershire.

THE PINERY

The evolution of the orangery led to further advances in glasshouse technology in order to grow the ever-more exotic and tropical plants that were being newly introduced, mainly from the East and West Indies. These included cocoa, coffee, bananas, and, most prized of all, pineapples, which reached extraordinary levels of popularity in the 18th century. Unlike the orangery, most other glasshouses such as the pinery and the vinery were designed as lean-to structures, called 'stoves', built along the kitchen-garden walls to benefit from the heat radiating from the brick.

Pineapples had come into the country in the 17th century as gifts to the monarch, and the excitement that the sight of these fruit generated is now hard for us to imagine. They were imported from the West Indies, but it was not long before attempts were made to produce them in Britain; such was the prestige of the fruit that whoever succeeded would no doubt earn great acclaim. In the 1680s

The King's Gardener, John Rose, presenting Charles II with a pineapple. This 17th-century painting by Hendrick Danckerts is an indication of the pineapple's position as the most prestigious fruit of all.

The prestigious pineapple was the subject of many books on their cultivation.

the Dutch had developed a hothouse suitable for growing these exotic fruit and in 1689 similar stoves were erected at Hampton Court when William of Orange acceded to the English throne. The innovative feature of these structures was the sloping glass walls, which were heated, ventilated and narrow, measuring 2.4m (8ft) from front to back to ensure all plants, even those at the back, received enough light. The first record of a pineapple ripening in this country was at Hampton Court in October 1703, although it is probable that the plant was raised in the Netherlands. Not everyone was a fan, however. Louis XI of France banned the cultivation of pineapples in France because, in his eagerness to try one, he cut his lip on the prickly skin when biting into it, too impatient to peel it first.

The first instructions on growing pineapples were published in 1721 by Richard Bradley in *A General Treatise of Husbandry and Gardening*. They require patience, taking up to three years to flower and producing only one large fruit and several smaller ones per plant. By the mid-18th century such was the status of the pineapple that those who failed to grow them could hire them as decorations for dinner parties, and as late as the 1920s it was considered that a party was really grand only if there were present both 'a pineapple and Lady Curzon'. In Georgian England the pineapple motif was used architecturally, especially on gate piers where it was a sign of welcome and wealth.

THE VINERY

Vines had historically been cultivated outside for the production of wine, but the increasingly popular dessert varieties of grape required indoor cultivation. They thrived in completely different conditions to the pineapple, so glasshouses were adapted for their specific needs. Although vines did not need year-round heat, it was crucial that the temperature did not fall below 10°C (50°F) during April and May, when they were just starting into growth. In the 1770s the first vinery was built specifically for the production of dessert grapes, and by the Victorian period gardeners would be expected to supply their employers with hothouse grapes all year round. The reputation of English hothouse grapes at the beginning of the 20th century was such that they were even exported to America.

An extensive range of fruit continued to be grown in glasshouses until the early 20th century.

Colour lithograph of a banana plant (1880).

LORD LECONFIELD'S BANANAS

Henry, 2nd Lord Leconfield (1830–1901), was determined to succeed in growing a banana at his Petworth estate in West Sussex, having heard that they tasted much better straight from the tree. He sent his gardener to Royal Botanic Gardens, Kew, to learn how to grow them, and, at great expense, equipped himself with everything needed for their cultivation including a 'special green house'. His grandson recounted the story:

The banana tree was splendid. My grandfather took a lively interest in its progress until, lo and behold, it fructified. 'I will have that banana for dinner tonight,' he said as soon as the banana was ripe. And so he did — amid a deathly hush. All were agog. The head gardener himself, controlling a great department of the estate, was not too proud to be there … Even the groom of the chambers broke the habit of a lifetime and turned up sober to watch.

The banana was brought in on a lordly dish, My grandfather peeled it with a golden knife, put it in his mouth and carefully tasted it. Whereupon he flung dish, plate, knife, fork and banana on to the floor and shouted, 'Oh God, it tastes just like any other damn banana!' Banana tree and all were ordered to be destroyed.

KITCHEN GARDEN ESTATE

Mushroom houses

The opposite of the light glasshouse was the dark and dank mushroom house. At Hanbury Hall in Worcestershire, the mushroom house is situated behind the orangery, making use of the cold north-facing back wall. Mushrooms were particularly popular in winter when fresh produce was scarce. William Taylor, the gardener at Longleat, Wiltshire, during the mid-19th century, wrote 'The Mushroom is amongst choice vegetables what the Grape is amongst choice fruit – it is indispensable.' The mushroom house also provided ideal conditions for forcing blanched vegetables such as sea kale, rhubarb and chicory.

The back sheds

These were usually sited along the north side of the south-facing kitchen garden wall, behind the lean-to glasshouses. They consisted of the boiler room (located below ground in order for the hot-water systems to work) and fuel bunkers, work rooms and potting sheds, storage sheds, seed rooms, bothies, packing rooms and the gardeners' mess room. Work rooms tended to be close to or above the boilers for warmth.

Detail from an archive photograph (c.1928) showing the team of gardeners at Polesden Lacey, Surrey.

The head gardener

A respected figure in the household, the head gardener held a very responsible role. He would have had great knowledge of the best gardening practices accumulated from years of experience and required skills to manage a team of staff, which might number up to 100 gardeners. Mr Pomfret, head gardener at Melford Hall in Suffolk in the 1920s, was one such dominating figure, dressed in a 'black bowler hat, a green baize apron covering the front of his black trousers and jacket, and a white shirt'. He governed the garden with such a tight rein that even the mistress of the house, Lady Hyde-Parker, did not escape his watchful eye. She recalled, 'If I took a peach from … the garden on a summer's day, Pomfret knew at once … he managed to convey that he knew perfectly well who the culprit was and that he disapproved strongly.' Such was the status of head gardeners that they were often forgiven a lack of the deference demanded of other servants.

Storing and preserving

Once harvested, the daily supplies for the kitchen had to be sorted, washed, trimmed, bundled, bunched and laid in barrows, boxes or baskets for delivery to the house. If the family were away the produce would be packed in hampers and sent to their place of residence. Produce to be stored required careful attention. The best apples and pears were placed individually on slatted shelves, while the second-rate specimens were packed in baskets. Thick-skinned acid cherries and plums, gooseberries and currants were also kept in the fruit room, still attached to their branches. Nuts and orchard fruit were stored in sealed, bran-filled jars in cellars or in beds of sand.

Cabbages, cauliflowers, pumpkins, marrow and onions were hung up in cool, airy roof spaces, and root crops such as potatoes and carrots could be stored in clumps of earth and straw outside, or layered with straw or sand in bins and kept in the cellar. In the summer, carrots, potatoes, turnips, beets, celery, cauliflower, peas and beans might be stored briefly in the icehouse.

A wide range of vegetables were pickled, for preservation and flavour: mushrooms, broom buds, beetroot, red cabbage, capers and samphire were preserved in vinegar, stale beer or verjuice, while cucumbers were boiled in vinegar flavoured with salt, pepper, fennel, dill and mace.

Fresh beetroot from the garden at Chirk Castle, Wrexham, bundled in a basket.

Modern-day kitchen gardening

Expansive Victorian walled kitchen gardens were a luxury afforded only by the very rich, requiring armies of gardeners to produce food all year round. The households were very large and food had to be provided for the family and all the servants, not to mention the lavish entertainments or sometimes royal visits. More modest households may have had smaller, simpler gardens but, with fewer mouths to feed, they were still able to grow a large proportion of their food, and this continued, certainly in rural communities, well into the 20th century.

Freshly picked vegetables in the kitchen garden at Knightshayes Court, Devon.

The need to be self-sufficient diminished as affordable food became widely available in shops and supermarkets throughout the country. Gardens were now reserved for precious ornamental plants. However, this has been at the expense of losing hundreds of years of experience in the cultivation of crops such as the best times to sow, how to prune for maximum cropping and what to do to manage pests and diseases. Most of all, what has been forgotten is the sheer unadulterated pleasure of biting into your very own fruit or vegetable, picked when perfectly ripe, still warm from the rays of the sun and full of flavour. This can never be replicated in . commercially grown varieties, many of which are harvested before fully ripe and stored for long periods. Luckily, the tide is turning and many people are eager to get back in touch with nature and grow what they can.

The potager

The traditional potager, where herbs and vegetables were grown for the pot, is a practical and attractive form of kitchen garden, based on hundreds of years of practice. It is most successful when flowers are included, as they attract beneficial insects and can also be cut for the house. Potagers are designed to be as ornamental as they are productive and can be surprisingly easy to achieve by following a few rules.

1. LAYOUT AND BEDS

Dividing the plot into quarters with paths in between makes it easy to establish a system of crop rotation and enables you to tend the beds without having to walk on them at risk of damaging the soil structure. Improving the soil is paramount to a successful kitchen garden, so a supply of compost and well-rotted manure are worth their weight in gold. Raised beds work particularly well and reduce the need for digging.

2. CROP ROTATION

Traditionally based on a four-bed system, crop rotation can also be achieved using a three-bed rotation with a fourth bed reserved for permanent perennial vegetables. An asparagus bed, for example, may take three years to establish but it is well worth the wait and easy to maintain thereafter. Perennial herbs such as lovage and sorrel need no looking after other than the occasional cut-back to produce young leaves, and will come back year after year. A handful of leaves makes a tasty and unusual soup.

Glass cloches protect tender vegetables in the kitchen garden at Arlington Court, Devon. The divided plot with paths between makes each bed easy to reach.

FOUR-YEAR CROP ROTATION

Plot A	Alliums	Onions, spring onions, shallots, leeks, garlic.
Plot B	Solanaceous (potatoes), root, tuberous crops	Peppers, tomatoes, aubergines, potatoes, sweet potatoes, celery, celeriac, beetroot, carrots, parsnips, scorzonera, salsify
Plot C	Brassicas	Cabbages, Chinese cabbages, brussels sprouts, cauliflowers, calabrese, broccoli, kale, swedes, turnips, radishes, kohl rabi, pak choi
Plot D	Legumes and pod crops	Broad beans, runner beans, French beans, peas, okra

In a four-bed plot only one bed needs to be manured each year, into which greedy crops will be planted the first year, the slightly less demanding crops moved to that bed the following year, crops that are happy in poorer soils grown there in the third year, and so on. It is sometimes difficult to stick rigidly to the system in a small garden, however, it is a useful guide. Miscellaneous crops such as salads and squashes can fit in where there is room.

The stately angelica adds structure in the gardens at Greenway, Devon.

3. ARCHITECTURAL PLANTS

Tall architectural plants such as cardoons (*Cynara cardunculus*), globe artichokes (*Cynara scolymus*) and angelica (*Angelica archangelica*) add structure to a garden, either as a single specimen or when grown in groups or individual beds. Sunflowers (*Helianthus annuus*) are also imposing plants. Although only the seeds are edible, they are worth growing to attract birds and insects – and for sheer exuberance they are hard to beat.

4. STANDARD BUSHES AND TREES

Standard fruit trees and bushes on slow-growing rootstocks add structure to the garden and can be pruned to shape. Cherries are now available on the dwarf 'Gisela' rootstock, keeping the fruit within easier reach than their taller counterpart. Standard gooseberries and currant bushes can be used to punctuate the overall design.

5. TRAINED FRUIT TREES

Trees fruit best when pruned and trained, and therefore lend themselves to being shaped as espaliers, cordons and fans. They make excellent barriers and edging, and pear or apple trees can be trained over an archway, making an attractive feature in the spring when in blossom and in the autumn when laden with fruit.

CORDON *A single-stemmed tree is planted at a 45-degree angle, tied to a permanent support such as a fence. It is an ideal way of growing several varieties in a small area.*

ESPALIER *Pairs of branches are trained horizontally along a support such as a fence at 45cm (18in) intervals. It is a decorative way to train trees, but not as simple to maintain as a cordon.*

FAN-TRAINED *This method of training a tree in a fan shape against a wall is especially suitable for cherries, plums and peaches.*

STEP-OVER *This historic form of training uses a single-tier espalier on a very dwarfing rootstock grown along a wire support 30cm (12in) from the ground. It is useful for edging borders.*

6. CLIMBERS

Wigwams, arbours and arches provide a vertical element and a useful framework for climbing plants, particularly peas, beans, gourds and squashes, along with flowers such as sweet peas. These features can be temporary and changed yearly, or used as permanent structures depending on their construction.

7. COMPANION PLANTING

Pests generally thrive in monocultures or where there is a limited variety of plants, therefore planting a wide range of fruit and vegetables means the searching pattern of the pest will be disrupted. Flowering plants are also useful when planted between crops, as they will attract predators to devour pests. For example marigolds (*Tagetes* spp. and *Calendula* spp.) deter aphids by attracting hoverflies, as do poppies (*Papaver* spp.), nasturtiums (*Tropaeolum* spp.) and morning glory (*Convolvulus tricolor*). Best of all, the flowers look great.

COMPANION GUIDE TO VEGETABLE PLANTING

CROP	GOOD COMPANIONS	AVOID
Apples	Chives, foxglove, wallflower, nasturtium, garlic, onion	
Apricots	Basil, tansy, wormwood	
Asparagus	Basil, parsley, tomato	
Aubergine	Beans	
Beans, broad or field	Brassicas, carrot, celery and celeriac, courgette and squash, potato, summer savory, most herbs	Onion and garlic
Beans, French	Celery, courgette and squash, potato, strawberry, sweetcorn	Onion and garlic
Beans, runner	Sweetcorn, summer savory	Beetroot and chard, kohl rabi, sunflowers
Beetroot and chards	Most beans, brassicas, onions, garlic, kohl rabi	Runner beans
Brassicas	Beetroot and chards, French marigolds, nasturtiums	Runner beans, strawberry, tomato
Carrot	Chives, leek, lettuce, onion, garlic, peas, tomato	Dill
Celery and celeriac	Brassicas, bean, leek, tomato	
Courgette and squash	Beans, nasturtium, peas, radish, sunflower, sweetcorn	Potato
Grapevines	Geranium, mulberry, hyssop, basil, tansy	
Kohl rabi	Beetroot and chard, courgette and squash	Potato, tomato, runner beans
Leek	Carrot, celery, onion, garlic	
Lettuce	Carrot, courgette and squash, radish, onion, strawberry	
Onion and garlic	Beetroot and chard, lettuce, strawberry, summer savory	Beans, peas
Parsnip	Peas, potato, lettuce, pepper, radish, garlic	
Peas	Beans, carrot, courgette and squash, radish, sweetcorn, turnip	Onion and garlic
Potato	Beans, brassicas, peas, sweetcorn, French marigold, nasturtium	Courgette and squash, sunflower, tomato
Radish	Chervil, courgette and squash, lettuce	
Spinach	Almost everything, including strawberry	
Strawberry	Borage, beans, lettuce, spinach, sage	Brassicas
Sunflower	Courgette and squash, sweetcorn	Potato
Sweetcorn	Beans, courgette and squash, peas, potato, sunflower, tomato	
Tomato	Asparagus, basil, carrot, onion and garlic, parsley, celery, marigold	Brassicas, kohl rabi, potato
Turnip and swede	Peas, nasturtium	

Forest gardening

For a less formal and time-consuming way of growing food at home, forest gardening provides an alternative approach. Although regarded as unconventional it is not new, having been practised in various parts of the world for thousands of years. Fruit was grown in layers in 17th- and 18th-century gardens, typically cherry trees underplanted with gooseberry bushes, which in turn were underplanted with strawberries. In the 18th-century landscape park, fruit was incorporated into the general planting of the 'wilderness' and as fruit-hedges.

This style of planting, which works with nature rather than trying to control it, is enjoying a renaissance in Britain. Robert Hart was an early 1960s exponent, when he trialled the principles of forest gardening on a small 506m² (600sq yd) plot. More recently, Martin Crawford has worked his 0.8ha (2 acre) field on the Dartington estate in Devon on the same principles for the last 15 years. Two of the advantages of forest gardening are sustainability and the no-dig, labour-saving, approach. The idea is to plant a wide variety of species each with a practical use, whether they are edible, attract pollinating insects or improve the fertility of the soil.

Because so many plants prove to be edible the possibilities are endless. According to Crawford, the dogwood (*Cornus capitata*) has fruits with a banana flavour; monkey puzzle and maidenhair trees (*Araucaria araucana* and *Ginkgo biloba*) have nuts that can be roasted or boiled. Barberries, the tiny red fruit of the *Berberis* shrub (grown as an ornamental in gardens throughout the country) were very popular with 18th-century cooks, who turned them into jelly for eating with mutton, or candied them whole for decoration on sweet dishes. Berries from the rowan tree (*Sorbus* spp.) were used to make jelly and the leaf buds of the common hawthorn (*Crataegus monogyna*) were called 'bread and cheese' because of the country tradition of using them as a sandwich filling. Wild native fruit trees that have been in decline in recent years would be equally suitable for forest gardens. Bullaces and damsons, for example, are easy to grow and ideal for making preserves and fruit liquors.

Rowan trees in berry in the Peak District, Derbyshire. The edible berries make the rowan tree an ideal candidate for the forest garden.

A successful forest garden is composed of the seven layers found in nature, from the canopy of large trees down through smaller trees, shrubs, climbers and vines, herbaceous perennials, ground cover and finally the root zone. The trees and shrubs offer a degree of shade and support for other plants while providing leaf mould to enrich the soil. There should also be plants that fix nitrogen in the soil. These include alders, broom, lime trees, elaeagnus, and false acacias (*Robinia pseudoacacia*). Equally beneficial are the herbaceous comfrey and sorrel which draw nutrients up to the topsoil. A forest garden will take a few years to develop fully and reward you with its bounty but for its 'pleasure and use' it should be well worth the wait. For more information on forest gardening see www.agroforestry.co.uk.

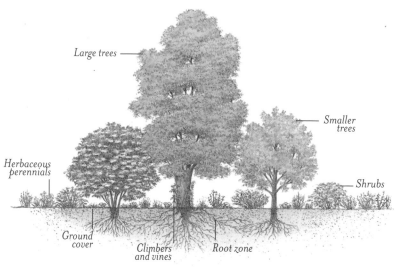

The seven layers of a successful forest garden include the canopy of large trees, smaller trees, shrubs, climbers and vines, herbaceous perennials, ground cover and the root zone.

Kitchen Garden Cake

175g (6oz) soft margarine
175g (6oz) caster sugar
3 eggs
225g (8oz) self-raising flour
½ tsp ground nutmeg
115g (4oz) carrot
115g (4oz) parsnip
115g (4oz) potato
115g (4oz) eating apple
zest and juice of 1 orange

TO DECORATE
115g (4oz) icing sugar
2 tbsp fresh orange juice

Preheat the oven to 180°C (350°F, Gas Mark 4). Cream together the margarine and sugar and beat in the eggs. Sieve together the flour and nutmeg and fold into the cake mixture along with the peeled and grated carrot, parsnip, potato and apple. Stir in the orange zest and juice. Turn into a 20cm (8in) diameter round cake tin and bake for 50–60 minutes until an inserted skewer comes out clean. Turn on to a wire rack to cool.

To decorate, sieve the icing sugar into a bowl then beat in the orange juice until the mixture is smooth and thick enough to coat the back of a spoon. Drizzle the orange water icing over the cake before serving.

Herbs and Flowers

I know a bank where the wild thyme blows,
Where ox-lips and the nodding violet grows;
Quite over-canopied with luscious woodbine,
With sweet musk-roses, and with eglantine.

— SHAKESPEARE, *A Midsummer Night's Dream* (1590—1596), ACT II SCENE I

The herb garden at Buckland Abbey, Devon, planted with over 40 varieties of herbs.

There are few sights that evoke gardens of the past more than a traditional herb garden – an abundant mix of angelicas, fennels and aromatic rosemary, embedded within ephemeral self-seeding mixes of violets, borage and marjoram to name but a few, all framed within a formal plot edged with a neatly clipped low-growing hedge. This style harks back to the medieval herb gardens of monasteries and manor houses, but is in fact a relatively modern interpretation originating in the 19th century.

Herbs have played a vital role in British gardens, most notably from the Middle Ages up until the landscape revolution of the 18th century. Their aroma would pervade the air, reinforcing the concept of the garden as an earthly paradise designed to engage all the senses. The instructions for making a garden as prescribed by the Dominican friar and scientist Albertus Magnus in the 13th century supports this idealised notion of the garden:

Certain gardens may be only of herbs [in the context of herbaceous plants], others with trees, and yet others of both ... let the site be planted with fragrant plants of all kinds, such as rue, sage, basil, marjoram, mint and the like and similarly all kinds of flowers, such as violet, columbine, lily, rose, iris, and the like . . . Beyond the lawn there may be a variety of medicinal and scented herbs, not only to delight the sense of smell, but to refresh the eye.

Borage, often planted among traditional herbs such as fennel and rosemary, will self-seed year after year.

It was not until the 18th century that the word 'vegetable' began to be used to describe a food crop; before then there was little distinction between herbs, vegetables and flowers, all of which served a purpose within the household. From the Middle Ages herbs were grown throughout the garden depending on their many uses, whether curative, culinary or cosmetic. Plants specifically for medicinal purposes would have been grown in a well-organised physic garden, culinary varieties such as parsley would have been cultivated in abundance in the kitchen gardens, and the most ornamental herbs would have enriched the pleasure gardens with their variety of fragrance and colour.

The sweet-toothed Elizabethans maximised the use of the flowers in their many dessert courses, crystallising petals to nibble as sweets and distilling the most fragrant flowers into aromatic waters to flavour desserts. By the end of the 17th century, inspiration derived from foreign travel, especially to Italy, elevated the salad, with its leafy mix of herbs, flowers and oily dressings, to king-of-the-table status in fashionable households, with endless variations being promoted as a healthy alternative to a traditional diet based mainly on meat and dairy products.

The Victorians grew a much-reduced range of herbs in their gardens; with the advent of commercially produced medicine there was little need to cultivate the healing varieties. This had an impact on the choice available for the kitchen. Bay, parsley, rosemary, sage and thyme became among the most commonly used and these remain in the staple herb repertoire today.

MAGIC AND MEDICINE

The powerful curative properties of herbs inevitably shrouded them in folklore. One of the most fantastical myths surrounds the mandrake (*Mandragora officinarum*), a highly poisonous plant mentioned in the book of Genesis as an antidote to infertility. The Romans were aware of its narcotic and hallucinogenic qualities, using it for pain relief. It was introduced into Britain by the middle of the 14th century, together with an ancient instruction for extracting it from the ground: the tap root resembles the human form, and it was long believed that when torn from the earth the plant would scream so loudly that it would kill anyone who heard it. In order to avoid human fatality, a dog was tied to the plant with a lead and then lured from a safe distance to a plate of meat. As the dog lunged forward, it pulled the plant from the ground. The reward for successfully extracting the mandrake was good luck conferred on the whole household. To compound this gruesome myth, mandrake was also believed to grow best when planted under a gallows.

Other herbs had more benevolent associations. Angelica (*Angelica archangelica*), a tall and stately plant, was named after an angel who appeared to a monk and told him that the plant was a cure for the plague; it had the added bonus of protection from witches and evil spirits. Heartsease (*Viola tricolor*), which had myriad colloquial names such as love-lies-bleeding and love-in-idleness, was supposed to mend a broken heart, while borage (*Borago officinalis*) symbolised courage; the little blue star-shaped flowers were floated in the

Canvaswork panel showing mandrakes derived from a 16th-century botanical plate book.

stirrup-cups of the Crusaders to send them on their way, a precursor to today's fashion for freezing borage flowers in ice cubes to add to drinks.

However, it was for their very real curative qualities that these aromatic herbs became indispensable. Before the advent of modern treatments they were the original medicines, many being used for more than one ailment, internally or externally and sometimes both. Black mustard (*Brassica nigra*), for example, was used to cure toothache and stomach ache, to ease asthmatic and epileptic conditions, to act as an antidote to mushroom poisoning and snake bites and, applied as a poultice, to soothe bruises and sprains. If it was to be taken internally, honey could be added to help the medicine go down.

Monks were particularly interested in exploring the remedial potential of herbs for use in the monastery infirmary, which catered not only for the monks but also the local community. In some establishments, special physic gardens were set up where herbs were grouped into specific types to be grown in geometric beds. Scientific discoveries in the plant kingdom were centuries away, so the medicinal virtue of a plant was based on the 'Doctrine of Signatures', which held that the appearance, smell or habit of a plant corresponded to a disease of the human

The delicate flower of heartsease in the kitchen garden at Ham House, Richmond-upon-Thames.

Woodcut (1542) showing a herb woman bringing collected medicinal plants to the doctor.

HERBS AND FLOWERS

body. Therefore a plant with heart-shaped leaves was assumed to be a remedy for a heart condition, while the spotted leaves of lungwort (*Pulmonaria officinalis*) were thought to cure diseases of the lungs. Self-heal (*Prunella vulgaris*) was used to heal wounds; its hook-like flowers resembled the sickle, a widely used farming implement and the cause of many injuries.

An increasing range of plants continued to be introduced by the returning Crusaders. Comfrey (*Symphytum officinale*) was one of the most widely used and earned the name of knit-bone for its alleged power to heal broken bones. It was also applied as a poultice to soothe wounds and bruises or as an ointment made by boiling the root with sugar and liquorice mixed with coltsfoot, mallow and poppy seed.

In an age of open sewers, herbs played a vital role in freshening the air. They were carried as little posies, or nosegays, to ward off bad smells, or strewn on the ground, their scent released with every footfall. Herbs were also useful insect repellents, no light matter in an age when fleas spread fatal diseases such as the plague. In a long poem entitled *Five Hundred Pointes of Good Husbandry*, published in 1557, the poet and farmer Thomas Tusser wrote:

While wormwood hath seed, get a bundle or twain,
To save against March, to make flea refrain:
Where chamber is swept, and wormwood is strown,
No flea for his life dare abide to be known.

Organic mint, marjoram, comfrey and tarragon growing in raised wooden beds in the west walled garden at Llanerchaeron, Ceredigion, reflecting the well-ordered beds of the medieval garden.

Herbs for the kitchen

Historically, herbs as part of the vegetable diet were consumed in a wide variety of ways – eaten raw in salads or cooked to impart flavour to meat and vegetable dishes, preserved as pickles and added to oils, vinegars, tonics and wines. Indirectly they lent their special flavour to honey, their pollen having been collected by bees in the garden.

There was a distinction between pot-herbs and 'sallets', or salads as they came to be known (see page 64). Pot-herbs, including borage, endive, parsley and spinach, were added to pottage (see page 14), whereas 'sallets' comprising a whole host of edible leaves such as chervil, rocket, sorrel and even orange seedlings would be eaten raw. Sweet herbs were those used especially to impart flavour in cooking, being pungent enough to disguise bland or rancid food. These included many perennial plants such as rosemary, sage, winter savory and thyme.

In the Middle Ages the range of herbs employed in cooking far exceeded that used today. The most common herb for the kitchen was parsley (*Petroselinum crispum*), a main ingredient in pottage and grown in great quantities, suggesting it was more than just a garnish on the side of the plate. Notoriously difficult to germinate, parsley was said to flourish where 'the missus is master'!

Sweet cicely (*Myrrhis odorata*) was among the most versatile herbs, being one of the first herbs to appear in early spring and almost the last to die down. All parts of the plant were used, including the lacy foliage, the frothy white flowers, the stems, roots and seeds. Its sweet, aniseed flavour complemented desserts and it was a useful sweetener for sharp fruit such as redcurrants and gooseberries before the widespread availability of sugar. The long tap root was served as a vegetable or, according to the 16th-century herbalist John Gerard, boiled to make an effective 'pick-me-up' or tonic. For household use, sweet cicely was rubbed on oak panels to make the wood shine and smell good.

Marjoram (*Origanum vulgare*) was used to flavour milk-based desserts as well as forcemeat stuffings. In the wild it grew by hill

Parsley, the most widely used herb in the medieval kitchen, growing in the kitchen garden at Knightshayes Court, Devon.

streams and was therefore considered compatible with fish dishes. Similarly, fennel (*Foeniculum vulgare*), said to grow wild along the estuaries where salmon run, was chiefly used to flavour fish sauces. An old recipe gives the following instruction: 'Melt butter in skillet, chop fennel till mist, stir into butter when it boils, cook two minutes and serve.' Lemon balm (*Melissa officinalis*) has, as its name suggests, delicious lemon-scented leaves that were added to summer drinks and the young leaves used in salads. Basil (*Ocimum basilicum*), a tender plant introduced to Europe in the 16th century, was grown in pots and according to an early herbal was said to 'be good for the hart and for the head. The seede cureth the infirmities of the hart, taketh away sorrowfulnesses which cometh of melancholie, and maketh a man merrie and glad'.

Other popular herbs were coriander (*Coriandrum sativum*), dill (*Anethum graveolens*), mint (*Mentha* spp.), mustard, sage (*Salvia officinalis*), savory (*Satureja* spp.), thyme (*Thymus* spp.), and watercress (*Rorippa nasturtium-aquaticum*), all herbs that have remained in use to this day. The delicate, sweetly aniseed leaves of chervil (*Anthriscus cerefolium*) were more appreciated in Britain in the past than they are today,

The enduringly popular spearmint growing in the cutting garden at Nunnington Hall, North Yorkshire.

although it remains one of the indispensable *fines herbes* of French cuisine, especially suited to white fish, asparagus or egg dishes. Less familiar herbs which were also frequently used included groundsel (*Senecio vulgaris*), these days condemned as weed as it is no longer considered safe to eat; langdebeef (*Picris echioides*) a pot-herb which is no longer used but is still known as the bristly ox-tongue, an anglicised version of its medieval French name; smallage or wild celery (*Apium graveolens*); nepp, also known as catmint (*Nepeta* spp.), now used mainly as an ornamental plant in the garden; and orach or mountain spinach (*Atriplex hortensis*), a free-seeding annual little used in this country today, though the red-leaved variety is still enjoyed by the Italians, who serve it as a substitute for spinach.

Alexanders (*Smyrnium olusatrum*), a popular herb with a celery-like flavour, was introduced by the Romans and widely consumed before the introduction of true celery. Although rarely eaten today, it can still be found growing not only wild in the coastal regions of southern Britain but also in the ruins of monasteries and castles, a tribute to its former popularity. If you are lucky you may find it on menus once more, evidence of a resurgent interest in wild food. Dittander, now more commonly known as pepperweed (*Lepidium latifolium*), a member of the mustard family, was another herb frequently found on lists of edible plants. Although related to cress, it is regarded today as little more than an invasive wild flower. Pungent herbs such as hyssop (*Hyssopus officinalis*) and lavender (*Lavandula angustifolia*) also had culinary uses, for flavouring oils and sugars and for adding to roast meats, although now they are valued more as decorative garden plants. The aromatic nature of all these herbs would have ensured a highly flavoured diet, contradicting the perception that British food was bland.

Lavender in the kitchen garden at Ham House, Richmond-upon-Thames.

RECIPE

An Herb Tart

'Take Sorrel, spinach, parsley, and boil them in water till they be very soft as pap; then take them up, and press the water clean from them, then take good store of yolks of eggs boiled very hard, and, chopping them with the herbs exceedingly small, then put in good store of currants, sugar, and cinnamon, and stir all well together; then put them into a deep tart coffin with good store of sweet butter, and cover it, and bake it like a pippin tart, and adorn the lid after the baking in that manner also, and so serve it up.'

GERVASE MARKHAM, *The English Huswife* (1615)

TUDOR AND ELIZABETHAN HERBS

After the dissolution of the monasteries, interest in herbs continued, with an added emphasis on their decorative possibilities in the garden. Matthew Parker, Archbishop of Canterbury in 1559–1575, described the role of his gardener at Lambeth Palace as 'to see ... that there be planted in the grounds flowers, hearbs and roots, both for the provision of the use and pleasure'. The idea of the geometric herb garden stems in part from the Elizabethan knot gardens – intricate plots resembling a knot, often defined with a low hedge. In his *Country House-wife's Garden* (1618), William Lawson, vicar of Ormesby in Yorkshire, explains their use in the garden:

The razor-sharp outline of the geometric 20th-century knot garden at Seaton Delaval Hall, Northumberland, is planted with roses and bordered by herbs, a nod to the gardens of the Tudor and Elizabethan eras.

'The number of forms, Mazes and Knots is so great, and men are so diversely delighted, that I leave every House-wife to her self ... and note this generally, that all plots be Square, and all are bordered about with ... Roses, Thorne, Rosemary, Bee-flowers, Hop, sage, or such like.'

The inclusion of flowers in both these accounts upholds the notion that beauty and utility were equal bedfellows in the garden. However, they were not included solely as ephemeral ornaments – they too were of value in the kitchen and around the house. No one embraced them more than the Elizabethans and their uses were infinite. Violets, primroses, cowslips and borage flowers were candied, and added to custards and tarts. The petals of marigolds imparted a pungent flavour and warm colour to other foodstuffs and were widely used by cooks to enrich the appearance and flavour of butter, cream and cheese. The yellow stain and honey aroma of saffron, the stamen of the crocus, enhanced savoury soups and stews and also cakes and breads. Now imported from the Middle East, it was historically cultivated in this country, most notably in Saffron Walden in Essex where John Evelyn vowed it was 'esteemed the best of any foreign country'. Roses were the most favoured blooms of all. Their candied buds and petals were eaten at banquets or served as a dainty snack.

Rose Petal and Almond Cream with Crystallised Rose Petals

This recipe was popular in the 17th and 18th centuries.

SERVES 6–8

175g (6oz) granulated
   sugar
300ml (10fl oz) water
petals of 2–4 dark red or
   pink scented roses
10g (¼oz) gelatine
a few drops of
   concentrated rosewater
squeeze of lemon juice
50g (2oz) flaked almonds
300ml (10fl oz) double or
   whipping cream

**FOR THE CRYSTALLISED
   ROSE PETALS:**

Rose petals
1 egg white, lightly beaten
icing sugar

First make the crystallised rose petals. Paint the egg white over all the surfaces of each rose petal. Sprinkle the petals evenly with icing sugar and then leave to dry on a cake rack, keeping the petals separate. When dry, place on greaseproof paper.

Preheat the oven to 180°C (350°F, Gas Mark 4). To make the cream, dissolve the sugar in the water over a low heat. Add the rose petals, bring to the boil, then cover and simmer for 10 minutes. Dissolve the gelatine in a little hot water and add to the rose-petal mixture. Add the rosewater and lemon juice and leave to cool.

Spread the almonds on a baking sheet and bake for 4–6 minutes until golden brown. When the rose-petal mixture has nearly set, whip the cream until thick and fold thoroughly into the mixture. Stir in three-quarters of the roasted almonds. Pour the mixture into a pretty bowl and chill for at least 1 hour.

Just before serving, sprinkle the remaining almonds on top and decorate with crystallised rose petals. If there are any petals left over, store in an airtight container in a cool, dry place – not in the fridge as they will go soggy.

A favourite of the Elizabethans, rose petals remained a popular flavouring in the 17th and 18th centuries.

Home distilling

The delicate floral aroma of roses was preserved for use throughout the year by distilling the petals to make rosewater. This would have been undertaken in the still-room, principally the domain of the lady of the house, and equipped with a furnace and a variety of stills for the extraction, or distillation, of the essential oils from every part of the plant, including the seeds, roots and flowers. Herbs were distilled for storing in the medicine cupboard. In *The English Huswife* (1615), Gervase Markham lists several uses: sage water was good for colic, angelica water for infection, celandine water soothed sore eyes, water of cloves eased stomach ache and washing the face in rosemary water would ensure a clear complexion, to give but a few examples. He also gives instructions for aqua vitae, a medicine or tonic made from a mixture of herbs and spices distilled with beer and fortified wine and taken 'a spoonful or two at a time' to derive the benefit from its infinite virtues.

Advertising scrap (c.1900) for Mason's Extract of Herbs.

The heyday of home distilling was from the Elizabethan to the Georgian period, when still-rooms were not only found in the households of the wealthy, but even small houses and farms. Sugary confections of all descriptions were also made in the still-room. The art of preserving and candying various fruit and flowers was considered a suitable diversion for a lady, although the high price of sugar at the time ensured that the sweetmeats produced were an expensive luxury enjoyed by the privileged few. In 1602 Sir Hugh Platt, an Elizabethan country gentleman who was interested in various aspects of gardening and agriculture, produced a book on instruction for the still-room, its full title being *Delightes for Ladies to Adorne their Persons, Tables, Closets, and Distillatories with Beauties, Banquets, Perfumes and Waters. Reade, Practise, and Censure*. Of all the delightful recipes given by Platt, one of the most ingenious is for candying rose petals on the bush by pouring syrup over them and letting them dry in the sun. This book was one of the most prized of all Elizabethan garden treatises.

TOP 10 EDIBLE FLOWERS AND THEIR USES

CAUTION: Use only clean, dry flowers that have not been sprayed with chemicals.

FLOWER	USES
Rose (*Rosa* spp.)	As well as being crystallised for decorating cakes and desserts (see page 61), handfuls of petals will also make a very pleasant jam. Alternatively, steep them in vinegar or dry them to make rose tea. Cut away the bitter white base of the petal before using.
Sweet violet (*Viola odorata*)	One of the few flowers available in the winter and early spring; both leaves and flowers are edible. Crystallise the tiny pink, white or purple flowers for decoration or add to desserts and fruit salads.
Sunflowers (*Helianthus annuus*)	Tall and stately, and one of the more substantial flowers, with buds, petals and seeds that are all edible. Steam the buds and serve like globe artichokes.
Pinks (*Dianthus* spp.)	Snip away the bitter white tips at the base of the petals of the sweet clove-scented flowers before sprinkling over soups and fruit salads or adding to sandwiches.
Marigolds (*Calendula officinalis*)	Used historically in dairy products and desserts, marigolds can be substituted for saffron. The leaves have a spicy flavour and the bright orange petals will enhance a salad.
Elderflower (*Sambucus nigra*)	The muscat fragrance of the tiny florets makes delicious summer cordials and 'champagne', a very popular drink with the flappers in the 1920s. Elderflower is a perfect complement to the flavour of gooseberries, which fruit at the same time of year, and a few petals added to apricot jam give a delicious twist to a familiar staple. Elderflower heads can be dipped in a light batter and deep fried, served with a sprinkling of sugar.
Chives (*Allium schoenoprasum*)	While chives are usually cultivated just for the leaves, the purple or pink pom-pom flowers enliven soups and salads when pulled apart and sprinkled over the top.
Nasturtium (*Tropaeolum majus*)	Add the peppery leaves and orange flowers to brighten up a salad. Pickle the buds as an alternative to capers: put in cold water and salt for three days, drain, then seal them in a jar of white-wine vinegar, chopped shallot, grated horseradish root, pepper, salt, cloves, mace and nutmeg.
Day lily (*Hemerocallis* spp.)	Traditionally eaten in Mexico and in China, where it is cultivated as a food crop, the flowers of day lily are crunchy and mildly peppery, adding colour and texture to a salad, or chopped up and added to stir-fries.
Lilac (*Syringa vulgaris*)	The highly scented florets have a lemony taste and can be eaten raw sprinkled over salads. Alternatively, batter them in the same manner as elderflower or crystallise to garnish a dessert.

A sprinkling of chive flower petals enhances soups and salads.

Salad days

In the 17th century the fashion for salads reached its peak. Increasingly complex combinations of herbs and flowers were incorporated into the leafy mix. In *The English Huswife* (1615) Markham offers up various salad recipes, such as preserved and pickled salads for year-round consumption. As far back as the Roman period, herbs and vegetables had been pickled to prolong their availability.

Cato, the Roman statesman and writer on agriculture, listed 'capers, stalks of parsley, rue, the flower of alexanders with its stalk' to be preserved using salt and vinegar and stored in jars. Markham drew a distinction between pickled and preserved 'sallats': pickled were boiled, drained and salted then pickled in water, salt and a little vinegar and stored in an earthenware pot, whereas preserved were combinations of washed and dried flowers such as violets, primrose, cowslip, pinks of all kinds, broom flowers and 'any wholesome flower whatsoever' added to an earthenware gallipot, or a glass pot, in layers alternating with sugar. They were then compressed and topped up with the 'best and sharpest' vinegar (preferably distilled to retain the colour of the petals). Once sealed these would last all year, to be eaten at leisure. Described as 'more excellent for taste than for to look on', these flowery salads captured the essence of summer and would have been especially appreciated during the bleak winter months.

Markham also described fresh salads, differentiating between 'simple sallats' of leaves or lightly boiled roots served with a little vinegar, oil and sugar, and 'compound sallats' which were 'the first young buds and knots of all manner of wholesome herbs at their first springing; as red sage, mints, lettuce, violets, marigolds, spinach, and many other mixed together, and then served up to the table with vinegar, sallat oil and sugar'. The spiralling range of ingredients resulted in the 'Grand Sallat', encompassing the garden on a plate, which was eaten either as a first course or as a light main course. The composition of this dish was all-important; the colours, flavours and textures of an elaborate combination of ingredients would be

Regimented rows of celery 'Galaxy' growing in the kitchen garden at Trengwainton, Cornwall.

KITCHEN GARDEN ESTATE

piled high on a large serving dish, with perhaps the newly introduced celery placed in the middle. Along with the leaves of various herbs and lettuces, more substantial ingredients were added, most importantly hard-boiled eggs, but other variations could include cooked beetroot, orange and lemon seedlings which were eaten like cress, cooked peas and potatoes, baby artichokes, capers, cucumbers, raisins, almonds, hams and fish, especially anchovies, and myriad other possibilities, all bejewelled with a variety of colourful flowers. By the 18th century this salad was given the curious name of Salamongundy or Salmagundy (below).

The 17th-century diarist John Evelyn travelled widely in France and Italy and was passionate about salads, comparing their composition to that of a musical score. In *Acetaria, A Discourse of Sallets* (1699), he pronounces: 'Every plant should come

Salamongundy or Salmagundy, an elaborate salad devised in the 18th century.

Salad crops growing in the kitchen garden at Knightshayes Court, Devon.

to bear its part, without being over-power'd by some herb of a stronger taste ... but fall into their places, like the notes in music.' Evelyn favoured simpler combinations of young herbs and baby potatoes, but curiously for someone who drew on Italian influences, he showed a dislike for garlic, arguing it was not for 'ladies palats, nor those who court them'. To dress the salad he recommended oil (preferably olive) and vinegar emulsified with an egg yolk, much as we might use today.

Evelyn prescribed every detail of the salad down to the dish in which it should be served, dismissing metal bowls which would react with the acid in the dressing, preferring instead blue and white 'Holland-Delft-Ware; neither too deep nor too shallow'.

DECLINE AND REVIVAL

The 18th-century landscape movement resulted in a separation of the aesthetic from the productive gardens, and the herbs would have been cultivated together with the fruit and vegetables within the walls of the productive kitchen garden and grown principally for use in the kitchen. While the therapeutic value of herbs began to decline as a developing interest in science led to new forms of medicines, Georgian households continued to be equipped with still-rooms where the herbs that were grown in the now increasingly obsolete physic gardens could be converted into medicinal and cosmetic potions. Certain herbs found their way into the ornamental gardens to be enjoyed for their perfume and beauty although they were banished from the kitchen. Lavender has certainly remained one of the most popular garden plants, its perfume appreciated not only in the garden but in diverse household goods such as soaps, polishes and toilet waters, and to fill sleep-inducing pillows.

By the middle of the 19th century, books on household management offered scant mention of herbs. In Jane Loudon's *The Lady's Country Companion* (1845) a brief paragraph in the vegetable section refers to pot herbs as being continually wanted in cookery 'and are much better planted in a garden near the kitchen'. She lists parsley as one of the most important and fennel, thyme, sage, various marjorams, winter and summer savory, mint and basil – the familiar core of herbs in use today. She also suggests drying sage and other herbs for storage.

The Book of Garden Management published by Samuel Orchart Beeton (1862) covers a section on 'sweet herbs', wherein it is stated 'A convenient spot in every kitchen garden should be appropriated to the growth of such herbs as are necessary and useful for culinary purposes. With a little care and management, the herb garden may be made not only useful, but ornamental also.' Also recommended is that each herb should have its own bed, with box or tile edgings separated by gravel walks, a prescription that continues to this day.

A backlash against the rapid pace and mass manufacture of the Industrial Revolution led

Rosemary, an easy-to-grow garden plant is equally useful in the kitchen.

to a reappraisal of practices and crafts from the medieval world, and elements from the herb garden were adopted as fanciful garden features. Springhill, Co. Londonderry, was known for its chamomile lawn, believed to have been planted in the 19th century when guests were invited to view the garden, the lawn in particular, before dinner. Once boots were removed the guests were permitted to refresh their tired feet in the soft and scented carpet of chamomile before returning, relaxed, to enjoy their dinner. Anyone who has experienced for themselves the delicious fragrance wafting from a chamomile lawn would not question this story.

This well-maintained chamomile lawn, surrounded by box, provides a centrepiece for the terrace at privately owned Cothay Manor in Somerset.

KITCHEN GARDEN ESTATE

Herb gardens were popular throughout the 20th century and are even more so today, with many books written on the diverse uses of herbs in both house and garden. They are easy to grow and attractive enough to adorn the most ornamental areas of the garden, being particularly well suited to formal compartments, edged with a tightly clipped box hedge where they can be separated into various categories, recalling the physic gardens of the past. Most are ideal for smaller gardens or for window boxes where they can be easily accessed from the kitchen. As several come from hot, dry climates they will survive with minimum water and thrive in pots. Happily the range of herbs available is once again expanding, as many top chefs are exploring the potential of long-forgotten wild species to add flavour and variety to our food.

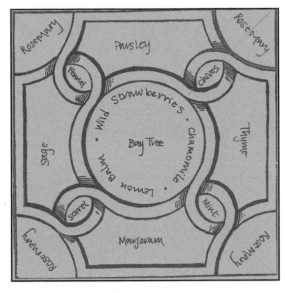

A herb garden based on Gervase Markham's early 17th-century design for an Elizabethan knot garden.

CHAMOMILE LAWN

A chamomile lawn should not be regarded as an alternative to a grass lawn except in very small gardens. It is not hard-wearing and requires regular maintenance to keep it weed-free, and an occasional trim, but when well grown it is a rare delight, appropriate as a centrepiece in a herb garden or courtyard (left). Prepare the soil very well by removing all weeds and ensure it is light and well-drained, adding grit and sand if necessary. The non-flowering variety *Chamomile nobile* 'Treneague' is the best for this purpose and as this variety has no flowers to set seed, buy plugs to plant at about 10-15cm (4–6in) apart. Resist walking on it for the first three months to allow it to establish. The same principles can be used to plant a chamomile seat.

Orchards

'No other fruit unites the fine qualities of all fruit as does the apple …
Its taste is sweet and it is extremely delightful both to smell and to look at.
Thus by charming all our senses at once, it deserves the praise that it receives.'
— PLUTARCH

The apple orchard in blossom at Barrington Court, Somerset.

Beauty and fruitfulness are attributes that have been associated with orchards since ancient times. They are one of the earliest and most natural forms of garden, embodied in Christian culture as the Garden of Eden. The notion of an orchard as a place for contemplation with biblical associations was adopted by monasteries in the Middle Ages, whereas for royal palaces the scent of the blossom and the dappled shade offered by the trees, together with the wild flowers growing beneath, provided an idealised setting for medieval romance and courtly love.

Orchards were both essential to the household economy and an integral part of the garden. This concept of profit and pleasure was espoused by many writers on gardens and rural affairs in the 16th and 17th centuries, and was portrayed in the frontispiece to Ralph Austin's *A Treatise of Fruit Trees* (1653) where two hands, one representing 'Profits' and the other 'Pleasures' are clasped together in unison.

Ideally two orchards would be planted, one for apples and pears, the other for stone fruit such as cherries, damsons and plums, although fruit was not the only provision of the orchard. The rough grass afforded ideal grazing, especially for pigs which consumed the windfalls of apples during autumn, thus adding a distinctive flavour to their meat. Bees pollinated the trees, maximising the harvest and producing an early crop of fine-flavoured honey.

Certain counties are particularly associated with orchards, especially in the west. In *Herefordshire Orchards* (1657), John Beale recorded:

Adam and Eve (1526) by Lucas Cranach, showing the apple — represented in Christian culture as the forbidden fruit — in the garden of Eden.

From the greatest to the poorest cottager, all habitations are encompassed with Orchards and Gardens; and in most places our hedges are enriched with rowes of fruit trees, pears or apples, Gennetmoyles, or crab apples . . . All our villages are in spring-time sweetened and beautified with the bloomed trees, which continue their changeable varietyes of Ornament til in the end of Autumn they fill our Garners with pleasant fruit and cellars with rich and winey liquors.

Likewise, Somerset was a county of apple-growing, in particular for the production of cider. In former times water was far from safe to drink, so cider and beer were the main beverages consumed by large sections of society, considered not only free of risk but beneficial to general health.

ORCHARDS FOR ALL

Orchards were considered beneficial to the population as a whole, harbouring none of the élitist associations attached to many exotic fruit cosseted in the walled gardens and glasshouses of the wealthy. Indeed, the cultivation of an orchard came to reflect Puritan notions of productivity and self-sufficiency. In 1655 Samuel Hartlib, an agricultural reformer and champion of the commonwealth, proposed a law to make the planting of fruit trees compulsory among the landowning classes, stating in his *Design for Plentie By a Universall Planting of Fruit Trees* that it would be 'for the benefit and public relief of this whole Nation ... for the relief of the poor, the benefit of the rich, and the delight of all'. Because of the downfall of the Commonwealth in 1660 his utopian ideals were never realised, but the idea of community orchards did not go away, re-emerging as recently as 1992 when the environmental charity Common Ground campaigned for wasteland to be planted up with fruit trees for the local communities. One of the first to be created was in Cotteridge, Birmingham, where a strip of disused allotments was being used as a dumping ground for green waste. In order to purchase the land for this community orchard, local people raised £7000 and have since planted it with 30 fruit trees. Similar examples are springing up around Britain.

A 'Blenheim Orange' apple tree in the kitchen garden at Barrington Court, Somerset.

FRUITS OF THE ORCHARD

In *Sketches of Rural Affairs* (1851), the anonymous author suggests the general stock for an orchard should consist of apple, pear, plum and cherry trees, although for 'a large orchard to be very complete ... it should contain quinces, medlars, mulberries, service-trees, filberts, Spanish nuts, and barberries, as well as walnuts and chestnuts'. Whatever the size of the orchard, the author insists that the larger proportion of trees should be of apple 'on account of their superior usefulness'.

Apples

Despite the diversity of fruit grown, apples are the fruit most closely associated with orchards. Although not a true native of this country they are well suited to the British climate and conditions and have come to be regarded as the most British of all fruit, and deeply associated with our culture, as Richard Bradley noted in his *New Improvements of Planting and Gardening* (1739):

There is no kind of Fruit better known in England than the apple, or more generally cultivated. It is of that use that I hold it almost impossible for the English to live without it, whether it be employed for that excellent Drink we call Cider, or for the many Dainties which are made of it in the Kitchen.

Apples have been bestowed with symbolism in classical, pagan and Christian cultures, their principal virtues being fruitfulness, prosperity and rejuvenation. The pagan ritual of wassailing – singing songs and banging pots – was believed to frighten away evil spirits that lurk in the winter orchards, and has continued as part of the New Year festivities. At Killerton in Devon the ritual is performed to encourage an orchard of historic Devon apples, such as 'Star of Devon', 'Devonshire Buckland' and 'Hangy Down'.

The native apple is the small crab apple, useful in cooking but not for eating raw. The larger sweet dessert apple is not native but is thought to have originated in central Asia. Possibly it found its way over to Britain with the Romans, who would have recognised the need to propagate trees from cuttings or grafting since apples rarely come true from seed, so complicated is their genetic makeup. The Romans practised many of the grafting techniques that are still used to this day, and they had more varieties of apple than any other fruit. The ancient varieties 'Court Pendu Plat' and 'Court Pendu Gris' are possibly Roman in origin.

The native crab apple used for making verjuice, once a staple ingredient in kitchens throughout Britain.

CIDER

One of the main reasons for cultivating great quantities of apples, particularly in the west of England, was for the production of cider. The 400 or more cider-apple varieties are testament to its importance as a national drink. Its heyday was between 1650 and 1750 when it was compared to the best French wines. In 1664 John Evelyn extolled its benefits: 'Generally all strong and pleasant cider excites and cleanses the Stomach, strengthens Digestion, and frees the Kidneys and Bladder from breeding the Gravel Stone.'

Cider was subject to regional variations. Celia Fiennes was not impressed with Somerset cider, thinking it inferior to that made in Herefordshire, as she wrote in her journal c.1690:

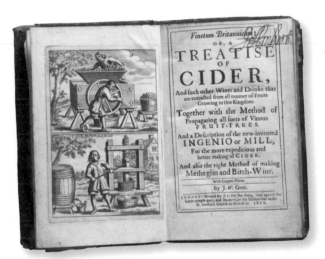

Vinetum Britannicum, or, A Treatise of Cider (1676) by John Worlidge.

In most parts of Sommer-setshire it is very fruitfull for orchards, plenty of apples and peares, but they are not curious in the planting the best sort of fruite, which is a great pitty; being so soone produced, and such quantetyes, they are likewise as careless when they make cider, they press all sorts of apples together, else they might have as good sider as in any other parts, even as good as the Herriffordshire; they make great quantetyes of cider their presses are verye large, so as I have seen a Cheese, as they call them, which yielded 2 hoddsheads; they pound their apples then lay fresh straw on the press, and on that a good lay of pulp of the apples, then turne in the ends of the straw over it all round, and lay fresh straw, then more apples up to the top.

Fiennes noticed that the best fruit was not used to make the cider, resulting in an inferior product, which reflects the thoughts of Sir Kenelm Digby, who in his 1669 notebook confirmed that 'The best apples make the best Cider'.

By the 19th century cider had begun to be produced on an industrial scale. Rather than using pure fermented apple juice, it was now made from watered-down concentrated apple juice from many sources around the world and artificially sweetened and carbonated. The inevitable decline in quality destroyed its reputation. Happily, as orchards are being restored, artisan producers are once again making cider from local and single-variety apples, elevating it to its former status as a great British drink.

Cider Syllabub with Bramley Apples and Hazelnut Cracknel

SERVES 6

300ml (10fl oz) medium-sweet cider

150g (5¼oz) caster sugar

¼ tsp ground cinnamon

juice of ½ lemon

2 large Bramley cooking apples, peeled, cored and quartered

30g (1oz) unsalted butter

50g (1¾oz) hazelnuts, roughly chopped

450ml (15fl oz) double cream

In a large bowl, mix together 150ml (5fl oz) cider, 50g (1¾oz) sugar, 2 large pinches of ground cinnamon and the lemon juice. Cover and place in the fridge until needed.

Cut each apple quarter lengthways into 8 slices. Melt the butter in a large frying pan and add the apple. Scatter with the remaining cinnamon and fry the apples for about 2 minutes on each side until golden, then remove from the heat (do this in two batches if necessary). Place to one side.

Place the remaining cider and sugar in a heavy-based pan over a low heat to dissolve the sugar. Turn up the heat and boil for 3 minutes, until clear and syrupy. Pour 2 tbsp of the syrup over the apples. Return the pan to the heat and cook until sticky (this should only take about 1 minute). Leave to one side.

To make the cracknel, put a sheet of kitchen foil on a baking sheet and scatter with the chopped hazelnuts. Put the remaining syrup back on the heat to boil. As the syrup starts to turn an even golden caramel colour, pour it over the nuts and encourage it to flow over the tray in a thin layer. Leave to harden for a few minutes. Break off medium-sized shards of cracknel for decorating and crack the remainder into smaller pieces to use in the syllabub.

To make the syllabub, remove the cider mixture from the fridge and gradually whisk in the cream. Continue to whisk, using an electric whisk, until the mixture holds its shape in soft peaks.

Divide the cooked apples between 6 serving glasses, scatter with the smaller pieces of cracknel and top with the syllabub. Chill if not using immediately. When ready to serve, decorate with the remaining shards of cracknel.

VERJUICE

Small native crab apples were frequently planted in orchards, especially in the hedges around the boundaries, to make verjuice. This condiment was used for cooking until the 19th century, when it was replaced with the more acidic lemon juice. Verjuice could be made from almost any unripe fruit; in France it was a by-product of the wine industry, where the unripe thinnings of the grapevine were used to make *verjus* – literally 'green juice', but in Britain the best was made from crab apples. One 17th-century recipe advises, 'Gather crabbs as soon as the kernels turn blacke, and lay them in a heap to sweat and take them into troughs and crush with beetles [heavy wooden mallets]. Make a bagge of coarse hair-clothe and fill it with the crabbes, and press and run the liquor into hogsheads.'

With the recent interest in historic recipes, verjuice is enjoying a renaissance among chefs today who use it especially for deglazing meat juices from roasting tins, and for adding a piquant flavour when cooking vegetables. In former times it was sometimes used instead of cider to curdle the milk when making syllabubs. Traditionally the cow would have been milked straight into the bucket of verjuice, as recorded in Kenelm Digby's book of recipes from 1669:

Take a pint of Verjuyce in a bowl; milk the Cow to the Verjuyce; take off the Curd; and take sweet–cream and beat them together with a little Sack [sherry–like wine] and Sugar; put it into your Syllabub pot; then strew Sugar on it, and so send it to the table.

Pears were more commonly espaliered than grown in orchards, as in the kitchen garden at Barrington Court, Somerset.

Pears

Pear orchards were cultivated mainly in the west of the country primarily for the cultivation of perry, the pear equivalent of cider. However pears were never quite as popular in Britain as they were in France, where the climate suited them better. A fashionable fruit nevertheless, pears were more commonly trained as espalier, benefiting from the warmth of the garden walls and consumed simply as a dessert fruit to be appreciate their delicate floral aroma.

Plums

Plums and damsons grew especially well in the west Midlands and the north. The prolific variety 'Shropshire Prune' was harvested not only for culinary purposes but also for the manufacture of dye used in the textile industry. Wild plums such as bullaces were also grown in orchards and can still be found in hedgerows or orchard boundaries, cropping very late in the season and well worth harvesting for jams and fruit liquors.

Cherry blossom at Bohetherick orchard, Cornwall

Cherries

Cherry orchards flourished in the south-east of England until the middle of the 20th century when commercial varieties from abroad affected the economic value of the home-grown varieties, most of which were subsequently destroyed. Kent was especially associated with cherry orchards, having an ideal sandy soil well suited to their cultivation and being close enough to the London markets to sell the fruit.

DYRHAM PARK, GLOUCESTERSHIRE

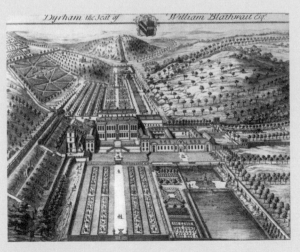

When the National Trust took over the estate at Dyrham Park in Gloucestershire, old pear trees were found in an overgrown orchard behind the church, which, together with the discovery of a brewery, indicated that perry would have been made on the estate. Records also revealed another historic orchard in the West Garden. This was restored in the 1970s with pear trees propagated from the original specimens and there are now about 40 trees of old varieties of perry pear in this orchard, such as 'Greenhorse', 'Blakeney Red', 'Butt' and an unusual variety called 'Swan's Egg'. The orchard produces up to a tonne of fruit in a year, which is once again being made into perry for sale to the public and for use in the kitchen.

Other fruit and nuts

Other orchard fruit would have included medlars, which are related to apples but have smaller fruit that have to 'blet', or soften, before it is ready to eat. Quinces, beautiful trees with sublimely perfumed golden fruit, were once commonly planted in orchards but are now rarely grown, possibly because the hard fruit is only useful when cooked. Quince dishes featured on the menu at banquets and feasts during the Middle Ages; for the coronation of Richard III in 1482, stuffed baked quinces were served, and in Shakespeare's *Romeo and Juliet* (c.1597) the nurse anticipates the nuptial celebrations, saying 'We shall have dates and quinces in pastry.'

Black mulberries were introduced in 1608 for the production of silk. However, since silkworms prefer the fruit of the white mulberry it is not surprising that the industry did not prosper. Despite this failure, the dark, intensely sweet fruit was found to be superior to its white counterpart so was planted instead for its fruit where, due to the longevity of the species, several original examples have survived.

Nut trees, typically planted to line walkways, were a traditional component of orchards and gardens, and still feature in many today. Dyrham Park in Gloucestershire has reinstated a nut walk and at Sissinghurst Castle in Kent, the 19th-century nuttery (below),

The Nuttery Walk in spring at Sissinghurst Castle, Kent.

comprising six rows of hazel trees, was a factor in Vita Sackville-West and Harold Nicolson's decision to purchase the property in 1930.

Wild fruit would have been planted in the hedgerows around an orchard. The 13th-century writer Walter de Biblesworth included hedgerow fruits in his list of fruiting trees that would have been cultivated in gardens, such as hawthorn, sloe, brier rose for rosehips, and cornel cherry.

ORNAMENTAL ORCHARDS

Descriptions of medieval orchards with their shady alleys and grassy walks studded with violets, daisies and periwinkles, together with the blossom and fruit of the trees, evoked an idealised paradise. In the 19th century this image was adopted by the Pre-Raphaelite artists

Alfred Parson's romantic vision, **The Pear Orchard** *(c.1903), with wild flowers and grazing sheep.*

who, weary of industrialisation, looked back to the values of medieval Britain for inspiration, producing a series of artworks featuring fruit and orchards, often as tapestries, a nod to the beautifully crafted textiles of the Middle Ages. A few years later the Edwardian artist and garden designer Alfred Parsons painted orchard scenes with billowing blossom-laden trees and swathes of wild flowers in meadow grass (right). These paintings capture on canvas the backlash against the rigidity of Victorian society, showing idyllic scenes that in a few years were to be largely destroyed by the ravages of two world wars together with cheap imports of fruit; by the middle of the 20th century two-thirds of Britain's orchards had been lost.

Traditionally, orchards were planted in a quincunx formation, like the five points on a dice. This shape represented the most efficient use of space, and ensured that from any vantage point the trees would always radiate away, retaining order in the design.

The emblematic orchard

The house and gardens at Lyveden New Bield, Thomas Tresham's early 17th-century garden in Northamptonshire, were designed as a coded expression of faith. The two orchards were very much part of the garden as a whole, surrounded by moats and raised walkways and overlooked by spiralling mounts. However, they differed from each other in their design and planting. The lower orchard was rectangular and planted with rows of about 300 trees, mainly apples, pears and plums with three parallel walks in between. There is also reference to a walnut-tree walk and a cherry walk. The southern end was bordered by the high terrace of the moated orchard which would have provided a view overall.

The moated orchard was the more emblematic of the two, consisting of a labyrinth of concentric circular borders with mounts at each corner to allow a view of the intricate pattern from above. Remains of Tresham's notebooks suggest that this orchard was to be planted predominantly with cherries and plums, together with standard roses and raspberries. Both orchards represented beauty and productivity; the lower orchard was very much a collection of trees, while in the moated orchard, Tresham, a devout Catholic living precariously in Protestant England, employed the labyrinth design found in the great cathedrals throughout Europe as a Christian symbolic device.

Sadly Tresham did not live to complete the house, the shell of which still casts a ghostly presence over the estate. However, the layout of the gardens has survived miraculously intact, despite the trees having been removed in 1609 soon after Tresham's death. To pay off the debts left by her late husband, Lady Tresham agreed to sell the trees to Robert Cecil of Hatfield House in Hertfordshire, who had described Lyveden as 'one of the fairest orchards that is in England'.

Analysis of the site, with the help of aerial photographs, has identified the planting pits where the trees would once have grown. This, together with what remains of Tresham's list of fruit varieties, has enabled the National Trust to restore at least one of the orchards as close to the original design as possible.

Aerial view of the newly planted orchard at Lyveden New Bield, Northamptonshire. Historically correct varieties such as 'Catshead' and 'Winter Queening' are planted in the formal grid of a traditional orchard.

KITCHEN GARDEN ESTATE

Apples for the kitchen

Fruit has long been acknowledged for its health-giving properties, but in the Middle Ages eating it raw was believed to cause 'bad stomach' and fevers. However, cooked apples, prepared with sugar and spices, would 'calm the stomach and ease chest pains', and were enjoyed by all levels of society. As such, apples were an important ingredient in the diet of medieval Britain, either as a dessert or served to complement savoury meat dishes.

New varieties of apples and pears were introduced to British orchards from France during the Norman invasion, although there were relatively few dessert apples available before the 16th century. One of the earliest named apples was the 'Pearmain', recorded soon after 1200. Another variety that was popular in the 13th century was the 'Costard', a very large apple that stored well and after which the costermongers, or London fruit sellers, were named, although the 'Costard' was later supplanted by a similar variety called 'Catshead'.

It was not until the Victorian period that hundreds of new varieties of apples were developed. The Victorians were also responsible for differentiating between cooking and eating apples, as they developed the idea of using specific varieties for particular dishes. This is well documented by today's authority on apples Dr Joan Morgan, who records that 'Keswick Codlin' and 'Early Victoria' produced a soufflé-like texture when baked, while the sharper flavour of 'Golden Noble' was perfect for pies, needing no extra flavouring from the traditional spices. Later cooking varieties useful for storing included the Victorian favourite 'Dumelows seedling', overtaken in the 20th century by the heavier cropping 'Bramley', one of the few cooking apples available in the market today.

Historic apple varieties grown at Berrington Hall, Herefordshire.

Erddig Apple Scones

450g (1lb) self-raising
  flour
1 tsp salt
110g (4oz) butter
50g (2oz) caster sugar
450g (1lb) dessert apples
milk, to mix

Preheat the oven to 200°C (400°F, Gas Mark 6). Grease and flour a baking sheet.

Sieve the flour with the salt into a large bowl. Cut the butter into small pieces and rub into the flour until the mixture resembles coarse breadcrumbs. Stir in the caster sugar. Peel and core the apples. Grate half the apples and roughly chop the rest. Stir into the mixture, then add sufficient milk to make a fairly soft dough.

Turn the dough on to a floured board. Knead for 2 minutes, then either cut into 12 or form into 2 rounds. If you choose rounds, score each into 6 wedges. Brush the tops with milk, sprinkle with a little sugar and bake for around 20 minutes.

SARAH EDINGTON, *The National Trust Complete Traditional Recipe Book* (2010)

CULTIVATING AN ORCHARD

The drastic demise of the nation's fruit-growing industry, together with a realisation of what has been lost, has provoked a rallying cry to plant orchards for the benefit of all once again. Orchards are a crucial wildlife habitat and one of the targets in the UK's biodiversity action plan as they are in steep decline. Old orchards are being restored, new ones planted and wasteland utilised for the good of the community.

A small orchard, defined by a group of at least five trees, is within the scope of the average-sized garden if dwarf rootstocks are used, five also being the ideal number for the traditional quincunx formation. A combination of different species of fruit would provide a household with a variety of fresh fruit from midsummer through to the winter if self-fertile varieties are chosen.

When planting an orchard, it is important not to neglect the ground underneath the trees. William Lawson suggested growing saffron, liquorice roots and other herbs for profit and flowers for pleasure so that no ground between the trees need be wasted, although he cautioned against planting too close to the trees themselves to avoid roots competing with each other. Long grass and wild flowers, with close-mown paths for access, will enhance any orchard and be an attraction for wildlife. The boundary of the orchard or garden will benefit from the inclusion of a few native hedgerow fruits and nuts, useful for making unusual jams, preserves and liquors.

The wisdom of planting regional varieties of fruit is generally recognised, since they have evolved to adapt to local conditions. Many counties have orchard groups from whom it will be possible to find out about the local cultivars.

Trees in blossom in May in the orchard at Nunnington Hall, North Yorkshire.

Rootstocks

Most commercially available trees are grafted on to rootstocks to control the ultimate size of the tree. Dwarfing rootstocks have been developed with the domestic market in mind, and have the added advantage that the trees will fruit at a younger age. However, very dwarfing varieties will need more fertile soil, regular watering and usually staking, and their yields are lower. Dwarfing rootstocks are now also used in commercial orchards because the fruit is easier to harvest and the trees can be planted closer together, but the increased density results in a reduced variety of plants at ground level, which can affect wildlife habitats.

Remove wedge from rootstock

Fit scion into place

Wrap union and seal with wax

Apples

Apples fruit from early August to late November, depending on the variety. Only a few, such as 'James Grieve' and 'Arthur Turner', are self-pollinating, so it is necessary for the majority to be planted with another that flowers at the same time of year. As a general rule, the early varieties are best eaten within a day or two of picking, whereas the later ones store well, even improving with time. Only store unblemished specimens wrapped individually in newspaper before packing in boxes or on shelves in a cool, frost-free place where they should keep until spring.

APPLE TREES ARE GRAFTED ON THE FOLLOWING ROOTSTOCKS:

M27	Extremely dwarfing, producing a bush only 2m (6½ft) high. Useful for growing in a pot.
M9	Very dwarfing – a good choice for a small garden.
M26	Dwarfing; slightly stronger and more vigorous than M9, needing only average soil and staking for the first five years.
MM106	Semi-dwarfing, or semi-vigorous, this is the most widely used rootstock, ideal for the average garden.
MM111 and M2	Vigorous. Too big for most gardens, but for a large area will grow into a good standard tree and is tolerant of poor soils.

Pears

Although once a highly regarded fruit, the reputation of pears has suffered in recent years because commercial growers harvest them before they are fully ripe, resulting in fruit that is too hard to bite into and lacking in flavour. However, anyone who has eaten a perfumed, juicy 'Doyenne du Comice' pear straight from the tree will understand the allure of this once favoured fruit. Pear trees respond well to pruning and are amenable to pot cultivation.

Pear trees are generally grafted on to quince roots. Quince 'A' is the most common, while Quince 'C' is less vigorous and suitable for cordons and espaliers.

Plums

Plums can be either of the dessert variety or used for cooking, a few being dual-purpose, most notably the popular self-fertile 'Victoria' plum. Greengages are generally the sweetest, 'Golden Transparent' having an especially good flavour. Damsons have a sharper flavour and are ideal for jam-making, while wild sloes (*Prunus spinosa*) are traditionally bottled and made into sloe gin.

St Julian A is the most common rootstock, suited to less than ideal conditions. Pixy is a newer dwarfing form with a mature height of up to 3m (10ft). Myrobalan B is very vigorous.

RECIPE

Sloe Gin

450g (1lb) sloes
450g (1lb) sugar
1 litre (1¾ pints) gin

Prick the sloes all over (traditionally this is done with a thorn from the tree) and put in a large sterilised jar. Add the sugar and gin. Seal tightly and shake every day for a week until the sugar is dissolved. Store for at least 3 months before drinking.

Sloes collected from blackthorn are traditionally steeped in gin for a winter tipple.

Edward Chambré Hardman's view of a cherry orchard at Roe Wen [Rowen] in the Conway Valley.

Cherry

Cherries are among the most beautiful of fruit trees, with profusely borne blossom in spring succeeded by glossy cherries and then vibrant autumn leaf colour. They are one of the earliest trees to fruit, usually ready to harvest from mid-June through to August, depending on the variety. Very few British-grown cherries are now commercially available so it is well worth growing one or two trees at home, especially the historic varieties such as 'Early Rivers' or 'Waterloo', the latter often considered to be the finest cherry of them all. Although most cherries are red, yellow varieties can be just as flavoursome, such as the Victorian variety 'Frogmore Early'.

The sour 'Morello' cherry is one of the oldest cultivated cherries still in existence

RECIPE

Plum, Apple and Pear Cake

SERVES 6—8
1 apple, peeled and cored
1 pear, peeled and cored
4 plums, stoned
175g (6oz) butter
175g (6oz) caster sugar
3 eggs, beaten
175g (6oz) self-raising flour
2 tsp ground cinnamon

FOR THE ICING
175g (6oz) icing sugar
1 tsp ground cinnamon

Preheat the oven to 180°C (350°F, Gas Mark 4). Grease and line an 20cm (8in) diameter deep cake tin.

Cut the flesh of the apple, pear and plum into 1cm (½in) dice. Cream together the butter and sugar until light and fluffy, then beat in the eggs. Fold in the flour, cinnamon and fruit. Turn into the tin and bake for 1 hour or until the cake is firm to the touch. Cool in the tin for 10 minutes and then turn on to a wire rack to cool completely.

To make the cinnamon icing, sift the icing sugar and cinnamon together and mix with water until a coating consistency is reached. Drizzle over the cake before serving.

and one of the easiest to grow. It has the advantage of tolerating shade, so is a rare contender for growing against a north-facing wall. Too tart to eat raw, it comes into its own when cooked and is the best variety for making cherry brandy. It has the benefit of being self-fertile, as does the sweet variety 'Stella', making these two ideal for smaller gardens. If you choose a variety that is not self-fertile it is important to plant a suitable partnering tree for cross-pollination.

Modern dwarfing rootstocks have been especially beneficial to the domestic cherry market; a restricted size makes netting the trees to protect the ripe fruit from birds easier, and harvesting the fruit is also more manageable. The Colt rootstock, introduced in the 1970s, enables trees to be maintained at 5–6m (16–20ft). Gisela 5 is an even more dwarfing rootstock, restricting the tree to a maximum height of around 2m (6½ft).

A TRIO OF TRADITIONAL FRUIT TREES

For those without the space for an orchard as such, a few choice fruit trees in the garden will give as much pleasure as any ornamental specimen, with the added benefit of fruit to eat. It is worth growing fruit that is not widely available in the shops. Three trees that featured in early English orchards and gardens are the medlar, the mulberry, and the quince, all of which have great ornamental merit and produce delicious fruit. They are easy to grow and self-fertile, so only one of each is needed, plus they require little or no pruning and are relatively free of pests and diseases.

Medlar fruit in the orchard at Lytes Cary, Somerset.

Medlar

Once the most common fruit of South West Asian origin, medlar trees (*Mespilus germanica*) have long been cultivated in Britain and can sometimes be found naturalised in the south and west of the country. This very attractive small tree with large single white flowers and good

RECIPE

Medlar Jelly

900g (2lb) medlars
300–600ml (10–20fl oz)
    water
sugar
lemon juice

Chop up the fruit and put in a pan with the water – the amount you will need depends on how ripe the fruit is. Simmer until soft then strain through muslin or a jelly bag.

Allow 450g (1lb) sugar to each 600ml (1 pint) juice and stir over a low heat until dissolved. Add 2 tablespoons of lemon juice to every 600ml (1 pint) juice, or 1 tablespoon if the fruit is firm. Boil rapidly until setting point is reached, then pour into sterilised jars and seal.

autumn colour can be grown as a standard, pruned to contain its size or left to grow in a charming haphazard manner, preferably in an open sunny site in well-drained soil. 'Nottingham' is a compact variety suitable for smaller gardens.

The fruit, shaped like a large round rosehip, is the colour of a russet apple and are not palatable when picked straight from the tree. They must be stored, calyx-end down to 'blet', or soften, for a few weeks in a dark, cool, frost-free shed until they turn a dark brown colour, rather like a date. Eat them whole with a platter of cheese, or scoop out the flesh and mash with cream and brown sugar, a traditional accompaniment to a glass of port. To cook them, arrange on a shallow dish with butter and cloves and bake for a few minutes. Medlar jelly (left) is a traditional accompaniment for game.

Black mulberry

Black mulberries (*Morus nigra*) were fashionable trees in the 17th century and very long-lived. In many historic gardens it is possible to find an old mulberry tree, its aged limbs usually propped up with supports, but nevertheless still bearing fruit.

The mulberry is a slow-growing tree; its gnarled appearance has a picturesque quality that complements a cottage garden. It prefers a well-drained, humus-rich soil and thrives in a sunny, sheltered corner. Grow it in a grass plot where the falling fruit can be easily gathered. Similar in appearance to a blackberry, the fruit has an intense sharp, sweet flavour, but is quick to perish, so is rarely found in shops.

Mulberries can be treated in the same way as raspberries, and are especially good as a pie-filling. In *Food in England* (1954), Dorothy Hartley suggests piling mulberries high in a

pyramid on a deep dish, sprinkling with sugar and baking lightly just until they burst and the juice starts to run out. Hartley advises to beware that the juice stains very badly, so it is best not to use your favourite tablecloth when serving mulberries.

Most children are familiar with the mulberry from the popular 19th-century nursery rhyme:

Here we go round the mulberry bush,
The mulberry bush,
The mulberry bush,
Here we go round the mulberry bush,
On a cold and frosty morning.

Although sweetly illustrated in Walter Cranes *The Baby's Opera* (1877), the rhyme is believed to have darker origins in the womens' prison at HMP Wakefield. A twig, taken from a mulberry tree growing at Hatfield Hall, Wakefield, was said to have been planted at the prison, eventually growing into a fully mature mulberry tree around which prisoners would take their daily exercise chanting this verse. While uncorroborated, a mulberry bush still thrives at the prison today.

Ripening fruit on the mulberry tree.

Four decorative girls go round the mulberry bush in Walter Crane's 'The Baby's Opera' (1877).

Quince

A quince at Berrington Hall, Herefordshire, in September.

Not to be confused with the ornamental quince *Chaenomeles japonica*, which has an inferior flavour, the quince *Cydonia oblonga* is an elegant tree with large pinkish-white blossom and beautiful hard, golden, pear-shaped fruit with a heady fragrance. Although not native to this country, it was well established in Britain by the Middle Ages. The fruit remained popular until the 19th century.

Quince trees are happiest in a sunny, sheltered spot in moist, humus-rich soil. Grow as either a freestanding specimen or, in northerly regions, train against a south- or west-facing wall. They rarely exceed 5m (16ft) in height when mature. Popular varieties are 'Vranja', which has large fruit with exceptional flavour, and 'Meeches Prolific', a smaller, earlier variety that keeps well.

The fruit is not eaten raw but has a delicate flavour and pretty rose-pink colour when cooked.

RECIPE

Quince Pie

This recipe is adapted from *The Compleat Housewife* by Eliza Smith, first published in 1727.

680g (1½lb) quinces,
    peeled and cored
100g (3½oz) caster sugar
1 tsp cinnamon
1 tsp ginger
1 clove
2 tbsp rosewater
150ml (5fl oz) water
225g (8oz) plain flour
60g (2oz) butter
1 egg yolk

Preheat the oven to 180°C (350°F, Gas mark 4). Place the fruit, sugar, spices, rosewater and water in a pan and simmer until the fruit is tender.

Sieve the flour into a bowl and rub in the butter. Add enough egg yolk to make a firm dough. Roll out the pastry to line a pie dish then arrange the quinces in the pastry and pour the liquid over them. Roll out a pastry lid and seal. Bake for 30 minutes in the oven until golden brown.

High in pectin, it is ideal for jams and jellies, either on its own or combined with other fruit. It is best known for *membrillo*, or 'quince cheese', not a cheese at all but a stiff jam-like paste. This delicious preserve is traditionally served with the cheese course. If you only have one or two fruit, they can be added to apple recipes for additional flavour.

Quince *ratafia* is a more unusual alternative to sloe gin (see page 85), and is made by adding grated quince and sugar to brandy, leaving it to infuse for several months. An alternative use is to place a bowl of quinces in a room where they will scent the air for days.

THE MOTHER ORCHARD AT COTEHELE

The National Trust's Cotehele Estate (below) on the banks of the river Tamar in East Cornwall has 5.3ha (13 acres) of orchards, most of which are apple, the remainder cherry. In 2008, the 'Mother Orchard' was planted as a gene bank of local varieties that have come under increasing threat as orchards have disappeared. This orchard holds 120 Cornish and Devonshire apple and other fruit tree varieties. With 270 trees in 3.2ha (8 acres), it is now the largest orchard on the estate. These trees will act as 'stock' trees from which the National Trust can propagate to disperse to the public and other properties in the region to secure the survival of these varieties.

Apple tree in blossom in the fruit orchards at Cotehele, Cornwall. Local varieties of apple are chosen for the orchards to help preserve trees which have been cultivated in the Tamar Vallley for centuries.

Bees and Beekeeping

'We have rather chosen to fill our hives with honey and wax; thus furnishing mankind with two of the noblest things, which are sweetness and light'.

— JONATHAN SWIFT, PREFACE TO *The Battle of the Books* (1704)

Beehives help pollination in the orchard at Sissinghurst Castle, Kent.

Few people today have experience of beekeeping but in previous centuries it was practised in cottage gardens and great estates alike, representing perhaps the most universal aspect of self-sufficiency in the garden. In the days before the widespread availability of sugar, honey was the principle sweetener used in cooking and preserving. It was equally valued for its medicinal qualities and for making mead, an alcoholic drink associated with monks in the Middle Ages. For household use, beeswax, produced by the bees to construct the comb for storing their eggs and honey, made the best candles and polishes – and, most importantly of all, bees are responsible for pollinating the majority of our food crops.

It is no surprise therefore that beekeeping developed hand-in-hand with agricultural evolution. Since earliest times humankind has been captivated by the mystical qualities of bees and their honey, the origin of bees being a particular subject of colourful speculation. One theory asserted that a swarm of bees could be born out of the carcass of a dead ox; another was that bees gathered their larvae from flowering plants and carried them back to the hive to raise as adults. What happened inside the hive remained secret until scientific revelations in the 18th century, yet it yielded one of the most prized substances for the household. Astonishingly, a single hive can contain up to 60,000 bees making about 23kg (50lb) of honey in a year, with each bee producing around a teaspoonful.

Honeybee feeding on a nectar–rich plant in the gardens at Coleton Fishacre, Devon.

Ultimately, beekeeping was a practical pursuit. The products of the hive were invaluable to the everyday needs of peasants and nobility alike. Early hives were inverted dome-shaped wicker or straw baskets called skeps, which would have been found at traditional cottages, farmsteads and manor houses, situated either within an orchard or in niches called beeboles in the garden wall (a 'bole' being a Scottish term for a recess in a wall).

Today, bees are making headline news as their numbers decline, possibly as a result of pests and diseases, though the cause has not yet been definitively proven. A world without bees is a dismal prospect for gardens, wildlife and potentially our own survival, since they pollinate over 70 per cent of the crops that provide 90 per cent of food worldwide. Not surprisingly, the nation has taken heed of the warning signs and many people are revisiting the idea of keeping a hive or two in the back garden. There is much to be gained from keeping bees, both for the benefit of the environment and as a direct way of connecting with nature.

Monasteries and medicine

The significance of bees to Christianity is represented in this copper engraving (c.1700) of a monk with bees and beehive.

Monks in medieval Britain would have appreciated the orderly and industrious nature of bees as an appropriate source of contemplation and a model for monastic life. Along with vegetables and fruit, monastery gardens would have been filled with an abundance of herbs for use in the infirmary, thus making them ideal places for bees to forage. In return the bees would have provided the monks with equally beneficial honey. Since ancient times honey has been recognised as an effective anti-inflammatory agent and has been consistently used as an antiseptic, especially during the First World War when medical supplies ran out; scientists are now undertaking research to discover if it might even kill the 'super-bug' MRSA.

The monks would not have wasted a single drop of honey. Even the little that was left in the wax cappings of the comb, removed during the honey-extracting process, was used to make mead, an alcoholic drink that had been popular since the Saxon period in Britain. It was especially beneficial for kidney ailments, gout, rheumatism, and as a digestive taken at the end of a meal. There were many variations of this health-giving elixir, including metheglin, a spiced mead typically flavoured with combinations of orange peel, rosemary, ginger, nutmeg, coriander, cinnamon, cloves or vanilla. Hydromel was a low-alcohol version, literally meaning honey water. In *The Closet of Sir Kenelm Digby Opened*, his personal recipe book from 1669, Sir Kenelm – a courtier and diplomat – lists no fewer than 100 variations (see box, opposite).

Beeswax had a special significance for the church and religious communities. Candles made with beeswax burned longer than tallow and smelled sweeter, but most importantly the wax represented the special status of bees in Christianity, explained in the early medieval Welsh Gwentian Code: 'The origin of bees is from paradise … and because of the sin of man they came thence; and God conferred His grace upon them, and therefore the mass cannot be sung without the wax.'

HYDROMEL AS I MADE IT WEAK FOR THE QUEEN MOTHER

Take 18 quarts of spring-water, and one quart of honey; when the water is warm, put the honey into it. When it boileth up, skim it very well, and continue skimming it, as long as any scum will rise. Then put in one Race of Ginger (sliced in thin slices), four Cloves, and a little sprig of green Rosemary. Let these boil in the Liquor so long, till in all it have boiled one hour. Then set it to cool, till it be blood-warm; and then put to it a spoonful of Ale-yest. When it is worked up, put it into a vessel of a fit size; and after two or three days, bottle it up. You may drink it after six weeks, or two moneths.

Thus was the Hydromel made that I gave the Queen, which was exceedingly liked by everybody.'

KENELM DIGBY, *The Closet of Sir Kenelm Digby Opened* (1669)

Other by-products of beekeeping that have been used for medicinal purposes are propolis, the sticky substance bees use to seal up any gaps in the hive, which has anti-biotic, anti-fungal and anti-viral properties, and royal jelly, a special food reserved principally for the larvae of the queen bee. Today it is used in skin creams and as a nutritional supplement.

Despite the dissolution of the monasteries in the 1530s, beekeeping maintained its popularity with the clergy. One of the most important books on instructions for beekeeping was *The Feminine Monarchy or a Treatise Concerning Bees, and the Due Ordering of Them* (1609) by the Reverend Charles Butler, a clergyman and practising beekeeper who became known as the 'the Father of English Beekeeping'. Much of what he wrote still holds true today.

The legendary healing properties of mead is depicted in Arthur Rackham's illustration from **The Rhinegold and the Valkyrie** (*1910*)

BEES AND THE COUNTRY HOUSE

The products of the hive were as vital to every household as they were to the church. As a sweetener honey was cheap to produce and available to everyone owning a hive. It was an ingredient in cakes and desserts and was also used in savoury dishes, for example as an ideal glazing for ham. Sugar was an alternative sweetener but, until the 19th century, was an exotic and expensive commodity, affordable only for the very wealthy. The preservative qualities of honey were beneficial to jam and pickle production. As well as many uses around the house, honey was also part of the rural economy, traditionally exchanged for rent.

An Apiary by John Papworth, from 'Hints On Ornamental Gardening' (1822).

The uses of beeswax

Beeswax was an invaluable commodity for historic households, having endless uses. Candles made from beeswax produce the brightest flame, and do not smoke but emit a subtle, sweet perfume. As such they were superior to tallow candles and used sparingly and only in the best company, especially after the instigation of a candle tax between 1709 until 1831.

Beeswax was particularly effective as a furniture polish and is still regarded as the best way to look after valuable antique furniture. Its natural waterproofing quality made it ideal for dressing leather, especially saddles, harnesses and shoes; it sealed letters and coated foods such as cheese to protect them as they aged, while in needlework it was used to stiffen thread, making it easier to work with, a device also employed by sailors to repair sails. For centuries artists have used wax to make moulds for bronze sculptures, a method perfected by the Romans.

In the garden beeswax was employed in the grafting of trees onto rootstocks, and is still preferred by many in the industry today. Beeswax continues to have many uses around the house. It will ease stiff drawers and windows if rubbed along the runners, and when screwing into new wood, first dip the screws into melted wax to prevent new wood from splitting. Prolong the life of iron hand tools by rubbing with beeswax to prevent rust, the wooden handles will also benefit from the added protection.

RECIPE

Beeswax furniture polish

Many of today's commercial furniture polishes contain silicone, which can have a detrimental effect on wooden furniture. Beeswax is a natural polish recommended for use on most hardwood furniture by conservators and antique restorers.

Caution: Wax is highly flammable and must not be melted over direct heat – always heat it over a saucepan of water. Use at own risk. Always test on a small area that is not usually seen before general use.

115g (4oz) beeswax
300ml (10fl oz) turpentine, warmed
15g (½oz) Carnubia wax (optional)
a few drops of lavender essential oil

In a bain-marie or a bowl set over a pan of simmering water, melt the beeswax to no more than 70°C (158°F). Remove from the heat and pour warmed turpentine into the wax, stirring thoroughly, until you have the right consistency. The addition of Carnubia wax, obtainable from bee equipment suppliers, will eliminate any tackiness, making the polish easier to use. Finally add a few drops of essential oil and mix well. Pour into small jars. Leave to set before adding lids.

HOUSEWIVES AND HUSBANDRY

It was customary for the lady of the house to manage the beehives and many texts throughout history address their instructions to the housewife. In *The Country House-wife's Garden* (1618), William Lawson includes a chapter on the husbandry of bees:

> *There remaineth one necessary thing to be prescribed, which in mine opinion makes as much for ornament as either flowers, or forme, or cleannesse, and I am sure as commodious as any of, or all the rest: which is Bees, well ordered. And I will not account her any of my good House wives, that wanteth either Bees, or skilfulnesse about them.*

Driving the bees from the old hive to the new in order to extract the honey combs, illustrated in 'The Pleasure and Profits of Bee-Driving' in Cassell's Magazine *(1883).*

One of the duties of the housewife was to extract the honey by 'sulphuring'. This entailed poisoning the bees by placing the skep over a pit of burning sulphur. The bees could then be shaken free of the combs, enabling the honey to be harvested, but killing the bees in the process. This method lasted for hundreds of years until there was an outcry from pioneers such as Thomas Wildman who, in his *Treatise on the Management of Bees* (1768) argued that:

> *Were we to kill a hen for her egg, the cow for her milk, or the sheep for the fleece it bears, everyone would instantly see how much we should act contrary to our own interests; and yet this is practised every year, in our inhuman and impolitic slaughter of the bees.*

The process was replaced by driving bees out of the full skep by drumming on its side. This would encourage the bees to evacuate the nest and crawl into an empty skep placed on top while the full skep would be emptied of its honey comb.

HIVES IN THE GARDEN

Early English books on beekeeping recommended keeping hives in the garden in an enclosure to provide protection from the weather, thieves and animals. John Fitzherbert's *Book of Husbandry* (1523), the first printed book to mention beekeeping, suggests that 'It is convenient, that the hyve be set in a garden, or an orchyarde, where as they may be kepte from the north wynde, and the mouth of the hyve towarde the sonne.' William Lawson's recommendation to the country housewife was that 'You must have an house made along, a sure dry wall in your garden, neere, or in your Orchard: for Bees love Flowers and wood with their hearts.' He also advises on the appropriate siting of the beehive, cautioning against the smoke from the brew-house or kitchen quarters, although warmth from the sun was desirable.

Lawson had an obvious affection for bees and admired the ornamental contribution that a well-managed apiary afforded the garden. In *A New Orchard and Garden* (1618) he advocates a 'Store of Bees in a dry and warm Bee-house, comely made of Firboards, to sing, and sit, and feed upon your flowers and sprouts, make a pleasant noise and sight. For cleanly and innocent Bees, of all other things, love and become, and thrive in an orchard. If they thrive … they will, besides the pleasure, yield great profit.'

Orchards were an ideal place to keep bees. The spring blossom provided an early crop of honey, while at the same time the trees would be well pollinated, ensuring a plentiful crop of fruits. By design, orchards are composed of a limited variety of species which gives the honey specific characteristics and flavour. Kitchen gardens were equally suitable since they contain a diversity of fruit, herbs, vegetables and flowers for a longer period, producing a later crop of flavourful honey.

In more modest homes, hives would adorn the cottage garden, prompting A. Pettigrew to mention in his *Handy Book of Bees* (1870) that 'a row of well-thatched bee-hives, all nicely clipped, standing in a cottage garden conveys to the minds of people passing by the idea of comfort and profit.' This sentiment is echoed at Blaise Hamlet, the group of 19th-century *cottages ornées* in Bristol, where, according to a contemporary, architect John Nash sought to reproduce 'all those little penthouses for beehives, ovens, and irregularities which he found in peasants' cottages'.

Bees delight in nectar-rich flowers.

One of the most exotic designs for a beehive can be found at Biddick Hall in Co. Durham. The body is based on a standard hive, but the roof resembles that of a Chinese pagoda (below). Not the most practical design perhaps, but a delightful addition to the knot garden in which they stand.

Plants

The term 'bee-garden' was first used in 1609 by Charles Butler as a place where bees were kept. However, by the middle of the 17th century the word 'apiary' was in use and 'bee-garden' often referred to a garden planted specifically with flowers to attract bees. Butler suggested the garden should be 'conveniently beset with trees & bushes fit to receive the swarms, as plumtrees, cheritrees, apletrees, filberds, hazels, thornes, roses &c'. Aromatic herbs were also attractive to bees, in particular rosemary and thyme. The Tudor nobleman Sir Thomas More grew rosemary in his Chelsea garden, which he endearingly 'lette ... run all over my walls because my bees love it', echoing the Roman Poet Virgil in his *Georgics*:

The privately owned Chinese-style beehives in the knot garden at Biddick Hall, County Durham.

KITCHEN GARDEN ESTATE

Let green rosemary, and wild thyme with far-flung fragrance,
and a wealth of strongly-scented savory, flower around them,
and let beds of violets drink from the trickling spring.

Phillyrea, an evergreen shrub of historic importance that has long been neglected, was considered by the agricultural improver John Worlidge in 1676 as one of the best plants to attract bees:

Above any other Tree, they [the bees] most affect the Phillyrea; one sort of them beareth in those Months [spring] an abundance of greenish Blossoms, which yield great plenty of gummy Rosinny Sweat, which the Bees daily transport to their Hives … Nothing can be more acceptable to your Bees than a Hedge of this Tree about your Apiary.

Many traditional cottage-garden flowers are attractive to bees, in particular the simple single-flowered varieties, as bees have more difficulty extracting nectar and pollen from the more complicated structure of double flowers.

A design for a bee-garden with a range of plants to provide both nectar and pollen throughout the year.

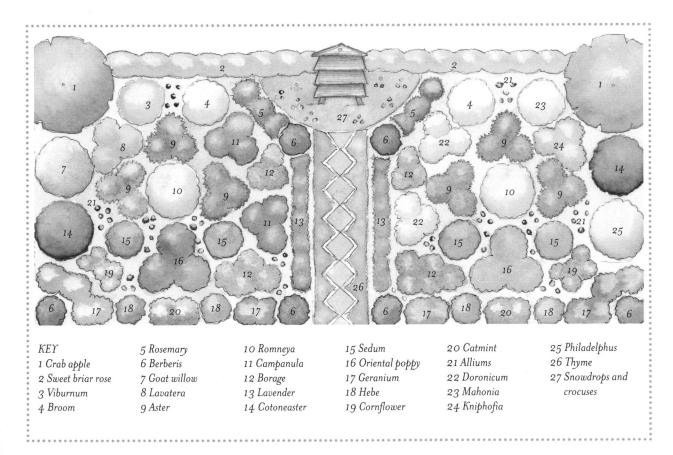

KEY
1 Crab apple	5 Rosemary	10 Romneya	15 Sedum	20 Catmint	25 Philadelphus
2 Sweet briar rose	6 Berberis	11 Campanula	16 Oriental poppy	21 Alliums	26 Thyme
3 Viburnum	7 Goat willow	12 Borage	17 Geranium	22 Doronicum	27 Snowdrops and
4 Broom	8 Lavatera	13 Lavender	18 Hebe	23 Mahonia	crocuses
	9 Aster	14 Cotoneaster	19 Cornflower	24 Kniphofia	

GARDEN PLANTS FOR BEES

Michaelmas Daisy (*Aster* spp.)

Aubrieta (*Aubrieta deltoidea*)

Barberry (*Berberis* spp.)

Borage (*Borago officinalis*)

Heather (*Calluna vulgaris*, *Erica* spp.)

Bell flower (*Campanula* spp.)

Cornflower (*Centaurea* spp.)

Wallflower (*Cheiranthus* spp.)

Cotoneaster (*Cotoneaster* spp.)

Crocus (*Crocus* spp.)

Broom (*Cytisus* spp.)

Leopard's bane (*Doronicum* spp.)

Eucryphia (*Eucryphia* spp.)

Blanket flower (*Gaillardia* spp.)

Snowdrops (*Galanthus nivalis*)

Cranesbill (*Geranium* spp.)

Hebe (*Hebe* spp.)

St John's wort (*Hypericum* spp.)

Busy lizzies (*Impatiens* spp.)

Red-hot-poker (*Kniphofia* spp.)

Deadnettle (*Lamium* spp.)

Lavender (*Lavandula angustifolia*)

Fried egg plant (*Limnanthes douglasii*)

Lithodora (*Lithodora diffusa*, syn. *Lithospermum diffusum*)

Mahonia (*Mahonia* spp.)

Apple (*Malus* spp.)

Mint (*Mentha* spp.)

Grape hyacinth (*Muscari* spp.)

Baby blue eyes (*Nemophila menziesii*)

Catmint (*Nepeta* spp.)

Marjoram (*Origanum* spp.)

Poppy (*Papaver* spp.)

Mock orange (*Philadelphus* spp.)

Cherry, plum etc. (*Prunus* spp.)

Firethorn (*Pyracantha* spp.)

Currants, gooseberry (*Ribes* spp.)

California tree poppy (*Romneya coulteri*)

Rosemary (*Rosmarinus officinalis*)

Blackberry, raspberry (*Rubus* spp.)

Willow (*Salix* spp.)

Sedum (*Sedum* spp.)

Stranvaesia (*Stranvaesia* spp.)

Thyme (*Thymus* spp.)

Viburnum (*Viburnum* spp.)

PLANTS TO AVOID

Euphorbia (*Euphorbia* spp.)

Mountain laurel (*Kalmia latifolia*)

Privet (*Ligustrum* spp.)

Rhododendrons (*Rhododendron* spp.)

Ragwort (*Senecio jacobaea*)

Lavender provides a valuable source of nectar for bumblebees.

SHELTERS FOR SKEPS

Bees have left an ornamental legacy not only in the plants of the bee-garden but also in the architectural features built to protect the vulnerable straw skeps from the vagaries of the British climate. These can be found as walls, stands and shelters in country-house gardens, farmsteads and cottages throughout the country. Many curious niches found in old garden walls today were once likely to have sheltered skeps.

Stands and bee-stones

To avoid contact with cold, damp ground, most skeps were placed on simple wooden stands raised about 60cm (2ft) from the ground. As these were uncovered the skeps would need to be weatherproofed. A coating of clay and dung would protect them from rain, or else a straw hackle, rather like a pointed hat, was placed over the skep as a cloche in the worst weather. Bee-stones were circular stone stands, usually with a projecting tongue for the bees to land on. A few of these stone examples have survived, though most wooden stands have long since perished. Nevertheless, wood was preferable to stone, which became too hot in summer and cold in winter.

Beeboles

Beeboles offered the best forms of protection. The skep would sit inside the recess, sheltered from wind and rain. In 1822 the landscape architect John Claudius Loudon recommended that the labourer's cottage should have 'a nitch in the wall of the south-east front of the house, to hold two or more beehives'. In *The Cottager's Garden* (1840), Loudon depicts a large ornamental gabled alcove with three shelves for skeps. This proximity to the household had the advantage that the activity of the bees, or for that matter anyone hoping to steal the honey, could best be observed, since honey was a valuable commodity. Some niches, especially in Scotland and more northerly regions, were flanked by small holes to accommodate bars which secured the skep within the bole to prevent theft. They also held in extra packing around the skep for insulation.

    Beeboles were also commonly situated in orchard and garden walls. The usual number of boles in a wall was between two and

six, though at Packwood House in Warwickshire there are 30 boles in the garden wall (left). Boles were set in rows or tiers, usually about 50cm (2ft) from ground level, and ideally faced south-east for warmth and early sun. They were found in every type of property, although the style of the boles would reflect the wealth of the owner. In 1908 Beatrix Potter used the beeboles at her Cumbrian farm as a model for the illustration in her *Tale of Jemima Puddle-Duck*. In larger gardens recesses called bee alcoves might be found. These were bigger than boles intended to hold more than one skep and, as befitting their status, were elaborate in design.

View of two bee boles set into the garden wall at Packwood House, Warwickshire, offering protection to the straw skeps.

Bee shelters

The most common way of sheltering skeps was to use bee shelters, which were either freestanding or, more often, a lean-to structure of shelves on which the skeps were placed. Although the majority of bee shelters would have been made of wood, most surviving examples are of stone, mainly found in the northern counties where they were built to withstand the harsher climate. There are more stone shelters recorded in Cumbria than any other county – at least 35 in gardens and two in orchards. An unusually elaborate Victorian stone bee shelter, originally from the aptly named Hive House in Nailsworth, Gloucestershire, can now be seen at the Gloucestershire College of Agriculture in Hartpury.

Bee houses

As the name might suggest, bee houses were little buildings entered by a door. Inside, hives were kept on shelves and bees entered and exited through a flight hole. These generous structures were found in large country gardens and date mainly from the 19th century. A ten-sided 19th-century wood and zinc lattice bee house made at Hall Place (now the Berkshire College of Agriculture) was situated in an orchard and housed skeps until the 1890s, when modern hives were installed. Attingham Park in Shropshire has a particularly ornamental bee house with a wooden lattice front (right).

Hives in buildings

Occasionally skeps were placed within houses themselves, under window seats for example, usually situated in the upper storeys of the building. The bees would enter via holes in the outside walls and travel through channels which led to their concealed hives. Evidence of this arrangement can be seen at the Nag's Head, a former public house near Avening, Gloucestershire (below). Bees entered through holes in a carved stone façade to reach their hive in an upstairs window seat. Even Varro, the ancient Roman writer on agricultural affairs, commented on hives situated in the portico of some villas.

The 18th-century bee house at Attingham Park, Shropshire, is not only ornamental; the wooden lattice would have provided light and insulation.

The Nag's Head near Avening, Gloucestershire. Its carved stone images of skeps have entry holes for access to the hive inside.

INNOVATIONS IN BEEKEEPING

Until the 18th century little was understood about the workings of bees inside their hives, despite various studies conducted by bee enthusiasts. As late as 1679, King Charles II's beekeeper Moses Rusden believed that colonies were increased by bees collecting 'the actual corporal substance of the young bees' from flowers. In an attempt to resolve the mystery William Mew, the 17th-century rector of Eastington, Gloucestershire, had the idea of designing a hive fitted with glass windows to study the bees at work. The model for this hive was passed to Dr John Wilkins of Wadham College, Oxford, who set one up in his own garden. Wilkins showed his glazed hives to the diarist John Evelyn, who described them as 'transparent apiaries which he had built like castles and palaces and so order'd them one upon another as to take the hony without destroying the bees.

These were adorn'd with a variety of dials, little statues, vanes, &c. and he was so aboundantly civil as finding me pleas'd with them, to present me with one of the hives.'

Evelyn treasured the hive given to him by Wilkins in 1654, keeping it in his garden at Sayes Court in Kent for many years. It attracted the attention of several notable figures such as fellow diarist Samuel Pepys and even King Charles II who, as Evelyn noted, 'fell into discourse with me concerning Bees &c'.

Despite such scientific studies it was more than a century later that there was a real breakthrough in understanding the workings of the hive. Francis Huber, a blind Swiss scientist, analysed the biology of honey bees and their colonies and discovered the importance of the internal spacing between the wax combs. The 'bee space' was a gap of about 6mm (¼in) that allowed bees to move freely between the frames and around the hive. His book *Nouvelles Observations sur les Abeilles* was published in 1792 and translated into English in 1806, eventually revolutionising

The lives of bees were little understood until the 19th century. Their hierarchies draw a parallel with British society in this illustration 'The Queen Bee in her Hive', published by G. S. Tregear (1837).

the way bees were kept with the invention of the modern hive by the Rev. L. L. Langstroth in the USA. Making practical use of Huber's studies, Langstroth developed rectangular frames which hung downwards, clear of the sides of the hives. This system allowed the frames to be easily removed to harvest honey and was introduced to Britain in 1862, remaining the basis for the modern hive in use today.

The first half of the 19th century is generally regarded as the golden age of beekeeping, with many developments taking place during this 50-year period. These included the introduction of comb foundation (a starter sheet of moulded wax which the bees draw out into cells and fill with honey) and the honey extractor. The design of the queen excluder ensured that the frames full of brood in the bottom half were kept separate from the frames full of honey in the upper half. In 1890 William Broughton Carr designed the WBC hive, a double-walled hive that has become the picture-book image of a traditional beehive. It remains one of the most ornamental hives on the market, but has been surpassed in popularity by the National hive, a single-walled hive designed in the 1920s.

The majority of hives are still made from wood, ideally Western red cedar, which lasts for many years without the need for wood preservative treatment. A recent breakthrough in the design of hives is in the use of modern materials such as polypropylene, which is light, durable and easy to clean. This, together with a new take on horizontally designed beehives, has resulted in the 'Beehaus' from the innovative company Omlet, also responsible for revolutionising the chicken-keeping market with the Eglu (see page 153).

BEEKEEPING TODAY

Increased awareness of the vital role that bees play in the ecology of the planet has led to a resurgence of interest in beekeeping, resulting in more local beekeeping societies and associations set up to help the novice keeper. Recent publicity about pests and diseases that are threatening the bee population have also encouraged many people to take up the challenge, in the hope that the devastation last experienced in the early 1900s when Isle of Wight disease wiped out 80 per cent of the native black bee population might be avoided. In order to restore original numbers after this episode, native bees were crossed with foreign varieties, and it is these hybrids that make up most of the bee population in Britain today.

A WBC hive in the kitchen garden at Biddulph Grange Garden, Staffordshire.

Getting started

The minimum that you will need to get started is a hive, a bee suit, time to make a weekly inspection during spring and summer and tolerance of the occasional sting. Equipment can set you back hundreds of pounds if you buy new; second-hand hives are usually available for a fraction of the price but must be scrupulously clean to prevent the spread of bee diseases.

However, before investing in any of the necessary equipment it is a good idea to have some practical experience, ideally from an experienced beekeeper who can show you the ropes or from a local beekeeping association which would give you hands-on experience and advice. Contact the British Beekeeper's Association for your local branch. These associations also run courses during the winter months, and most will hire out expensive equipment such as honey extractors. To see beekeeping practised in a traditional environment, contact National Trust properties near you as many are encouraging beekeepers to site apiaries in their gardens, as they would have done in the past.

EQUIPMENT

The basic starting equipment is a hive equipped with frames of wax foundation in both the brood box (where the eggs are hatched) and the super (the box reserved for honey which is to be harvested), as well as a queen excluder, which prevents the queen from laying eggs in the super. Most people opt for the National hive, being simpler to use and widely available. The double wall system of the WBC has the advantage of providing insulation and added protection from woodpeckers, but to its detriment there is more to remove when inspecting the hive. Most importantly, whichever one you choose, stick with that type since you are likely to acquire several hives as your colonies increase and you may need to interchange parts.

Along with your hive you will need a smoker to pacify the bees, a hive tool to manipulate the frames, and – essential for the beginner – a bee suit and gloves to protect you from the inevitable occasional sting. Most of the other equipment you will need, such as extractors for harvesting the honey, can be hired, borrowed or purchased at a later date.

You can start with a swarm of bees that has been collected locally, but as the provenance will be unknown it is better to buy a nucleus of bees from an established beekeeper or bee-supplies shop, delivered in early summer. This will enable you to build up the colony and you may even be rewarded with enough honey to harvest at the end of your first season.

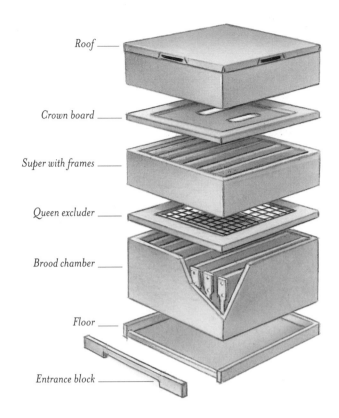

Roof

Crown board

Super with frames

Queen excluder

Brood chamber

Floor

Entrance block

A National hive and its component parts.

Siting the hive

It is essential to site the hive in a permanent position before your bees arrive, as moving it once full is not a simple task; bees have strong homing instincts and if you move the hive more than about 1.5m (5ft) they will become disoriented, so it is best to do it in small stages. Ideally, place your hive in a sunny sheltered site, away from neighbours and public rights of way. To ensure the bees fly high,

Well-protected beekeepers in the gardens at Felbrigg Hall, Norfolk.

have the entrance facing a 2m (6½ft) hedge or fence which the bees will fly over and out of the way of human activity. Although bees kept in gardens have the advantage of flowers at close range, most foraging takes place further away within 5km (3 miles) of the hive.

Annual tasks

The beekeeping year starts in spring, usually March, when early blossoms encourage the bees into action. It will be necessary to check the weight of the hive by giving it a gentle heft to ensure there are sufficient food stocks. If in doubt, give a feed of sugar syrup.

In April, if the weather is warm enough, it may be possible to inspect the hive to check for evidence of a laying queen and to ensure all is well. Each colony will have just one queen, distinguishable by her pointed abdomen and her size – she is much bigger than the other bees. If you are unable to see the queen, check the frames for eggs and larvae that prove she is present. You will also notice cells of worker bees (who do all the foraging and cleaning of the hive) and the larger drones, whose only purpose is to mate with the queen. If you have not done so already you will want to add a super on top of the brood for the bees to fill with honey. If oilseed rape is flowering locally, be prepared for an early harvest and extract the capped honey immediately, as oilseed rape honey sets very quickly. During May and June the bees will be very active and are likely to prepare to swarm. You will have to be vigilant and undertake whichever swarm-prevention method you have chosen.

July and August are the months to extract the bulk of the honey, ensuring there is enough left in the hive to feed the bees throughout the winter. Once the honey has been extracted it is essential that you treat the colony for varroa mite, which is one of the major threats to bees today. While it cannot as yet be eliminated from the bee population, controlling it is a vital part of modern-day beekeeping. In September and October, feed the bees sugar syrup to replenish their stores if necessary and put the hive to bed for the winter.

Natural beekeeping

Currently, alternative ways of keeping bees are being explored. Pioneers such as Phil Chandler, who take their lead from the lifestyle of wild bees, attribute many of the problems faced by bees today to excessive human interference in their management. Unlike conventional beekeeping, the natural method does not involve clipping the queen's wings to prevent swarming, and a fine spray of water mimicking rain is used to calm the bees rather than smoking them, which signals to them that their house is on fire. Minimal interference with the hive is the key to natural beekeeping, thus avoiding regular inspections which can cool the hive to a temperature that suits the varroa mite. The beehives themselves are more akin to the skeps of old than the sophisticated modern beehive, and most are home-made, costing very little. The bees are left to create their own comb as they would do in the wild and are allowed to swarm. One downside of this method is that it is unlikely to produce as much honey as conventional methods, so it is not a commercially viable option but may suit the amateur who prefers a less invasive approach.

Apple blossom and honey bee in the fruit orchards at Cotehele, Cornwall.

RECIPE

Honeyed Pears with Mead

8 ripe pears, peeled
  and cored
225g (8oz) unsalted butter
4 glasses mead
8 tbsp runny honey
8 scoops dairy ice cream
pinch of freshly grated
  nutmeg

Slice a little off the bottom of the pears so that they will sit on the plate. Melt the butter in a pan, add the pears and cook for 7–8 minutes over a medium heat, cooking the fruit evenly and gently.

When the pears are golden brown, pour the mead over them and simmer to reduce the liquid. Arrange the pears on a plate, drizzle the honey over and serve with a quenelle of ice cream on the side and a dusting of nutmeg.

Fish Ponds and Lakes

'Of all nations and countries, England is best served of Fysshe not only of all manner of sea-fysshe, but also of fresh-water fysshe, and of all manner of sorts of salt-fysshe.'

— ANDREW BOORDE, *A Dyetary of Helth* (1542)

Sunset over the lake at Croome Park, Worcestershire. The reflective quality of a naturalistic stretch of water was used to enhance the landscape park.

Not surprisingly for an island nation, fish and the catching of them have featured prominently in the history of Britain, not only in our seas and rivers but also in the ponds and lakes of our country-house gardens. These water features were frequently recorded by country-house visitors in past centuries, yet surprisingly they have until recently been largely overlooked by the chroniclers of garden history.

Pond-making has an ancient history going back thousands of years, with the Romans developing the idea of fish ponds initially to be able to keep sea fish inland. The Roman statesman Cassiodorus declared that the sight of a fish pond 'both refreshes the spirit with pleasure and charms the eye with wonder'. The Romans introduced pond-making technology to Britain but it was not until the medieval period, when the powerful monastic communities were especially reliant on fish to supplement their diet, that the construction of large-scale fish ponds began in earnest. At the time, a regular supply of fresh fish would only have been available to people living near the sea; most of the catch was preserved by salting, smoking or pickling and was regarded as peasant food. Freshwater fish could be caught from rivers but it was a time-consuming and unreliable way to feed a household, so for inland regions rearing fish in ponds was the ideal solution.

The ornamental lake was a prerequisite of the 18th-century landscape park as shown in this view of Dudmaston in Shropshire (1793).

As building ponds would have been an expensive business they, together with deer parks and dovecotes, came to be regarded as a status symbol. Over the centuries, many ponds evolved into elaborate formal water gardens and eventually into the naturalistic lakes of the 18th-century landscape park, where the wealthy landowning families could safely enjoy sailing while fishing for their supper or to offer their catch as a gift to friends and neighbours. Tourists to country houses in the 17th and 18th centuries invariably commented on the fish ponds and the varieties of fish they contained with the same enthusiasm as other ornamental features of the garden. Fishing pavilions and boat-houses evolved into architectural embellishments at the waters' edge.

INNOVATION AND DESIGN

Some of the most impressive medieval fish ponds can be found at Fountains Abbey in Yorkshire, and the clue is in the name: an 8ha (20 acre) area called Pondgate, strategically situated beyond the kitchens, which comprised a series of ponds. However, the rearing of fish was not necessarily confined to fish ponds; it could take place in any existing water around the estate, such as mill ponds or moats. The mill pond at Fountains Abbey would have contained plenty of eel, a popular fish that would have been available to the wider population. At Speke Hall near Liverpool there are references to the moat being stocked with carp and perch in 1693. However, a word of warning was given by the physician Andrew Boorde in his *Dyetary of Helth* (1542) which cautioned 'let not the filth of the kitchen descend in the moat' for fear it might contaminate the fish.

Fish could be kept in moats and mill ponds, as at Fountains Mill on Fountains Abbey estate, North Yorkshire.

The ideal situation was to rear fish in a series of specially designed ponds, usually formed by placing earth dams across narrow valleys, with sluices to control the water. There were ponds where fish were bred and fattened, which needed to be drained on a regular basis in order to separate the fish that were too small for eating. These would be returned to the pond to grow, while those that were big enough for the table were transferred to the cleaner water of the stew ponds, sited closer to the house, where the fish would be purged of mud until required by the cook. In *A Discourse of Fish and Fish Ponds* (1713), the landowner Roger North advised positioning the stew ponds near the kitchen for security and ease of access, commenting as well on their ornamental attributes:

The peculiar use of these is to maintain fish for daily use of your House and Friends, whereby you may with little Trouble, and at any Time, take out all or any Fish they contain; therefore it is good to place them in some inclos'd Grounds, near the chief Mansion-House. Some recess in a garden is very proper, because the Fish are fenc'd from Robbers, and your journey to them is short and easy, and your Eye will often be upon them, which will conduce to their being well kept, and they will be an ornament to the Walks.

Fish ponds were invariably square or oblong in shape and their considerable size would have ensured they were a prominent feature of the estate; North proposes three ponds for a 6ha (15 acre) area and two ponds for 3ha (8 acres). Although fish ponds are usually associated with pre-industrial self-sufficiency, they continued to be built well into the 19th century in middle-class gardens. In *The Lady's Country Companion* (1845) Jane Loudon describes the various forms of pond appropriate for different fish, and in line with the aesthetics of the day she distinguishes between ponds for the ornamental garden and those that were purely utilitarian: when the pond is in view of the house she recommends that the outline 'should either be varied, or broken by planting trees or shrubs in small groups on its banks' and alternatively, 'Where ponds are intended solely for fish, without regard to their appearance in the landscape, their banks should be quite straight and their shape square or oblong.'

Although thousands of ponds would have been built in the grounds of country houses, it is unusual to find original surviving examples, as most were eventually filled in. However, there are a few examples that have slipped through the net. Baddesley Clinton in Warwickshire has the remains of a chain of ponds linked by sluices that date from 1444 (below) and at Horton Court in South Gloucestershire one pond from a series of very early Norman ponds survives. Hardwick Hall in Derbyshire has an impressive series of ponds near the old Hall, now used by local fishing groups.

One of the fish pools at Baddesley Clinton, Warwickshire, used to provide fresh fish to the household.

USE AND BEAUTY

Before the 18th-century garden revolution that divided the ornamental and the food-growing areas of the garden, ponds would have been designed for maximum productivity and equally as an adornment. Ideally, there should be upper and lower ponds, so that, according to North, 'the Point of the lower, may also reach the Head or Bank of the upper; which will be very beautiful as well as profitable'. Celia Fiennes, that intrepid traveller of the late 17th century, described such a formation of fish ponds on a visit to Woburn Abbey, Bedfordshire in 1697 where the ponds were 'on the flats ... the whole length of the walk; above that in the next flat is 2 fish ponds'. These ponds were evidently part of the garden tour, designed to impress visitors.

Ponds became increasingly stylised, presented as moats and canals and surrounded by raised walkways to show off the design to best advantage. A plan of fish ponds from Gervase Markham's *Cheape and Good Husbandry* (1631) shows:

Deep pink water lillies enhance the ornamental qualities of the water at Bodnant Garden, Conwy.

A Platforme for Ponds ... for the better satisfaction and delight of such as having a convenient plot of ground for the same purpose shall be desirous to make any Ponds for the increase and store of Fish ... The Walks about the Ponds may be planted with Fruite-trees or Willowes.

The plan is in the geometric style of the period with ponds flanking either side of a central walk, and further grass walks around the ponds. Water gardens of this period were generally divided into separate ponds to retain the various regimes of keeping fish while taking on a more elaborate design. Islands situated within the ponds were a typical feature of this style, having the advantage of attracting nesting wildfowl – another source of food. These water gardens were a nod to the skilled Dutch water engineers who had been brought over to Britain to work on land-drainage projects at around this time.

The 17th-century water
garden at Westbury Court,
Gloucestershire, showing the
Dutch-influenced canals
with the pavilion beyond.

Few water gardens from this period survive. Research of the
remains of a water garden at Tackley in Oxfordshire has revealed
a layout very similar to the one described by Markham, including a
mount from which the gardens could be best appreciated. Mounts
had been a feature of gardens since the Tudor period but their
frequent association with ponds suggest they were a convenient way
to dispose of the spoil that had been dug out to create the pond. At
Lyveden New Bield, Thomas Tresham's lodge in Northamptonshire,
the restoration of a rare and early surviving garden from the end of
the 16th century gives the visitor a unique experience. It appears to
be based on the medieval moated pattern with mounts and raised
walkways alongside the moats which surrounded a grand orchard,
now happily reinstated (see page 80).

The Dutch influence was particularly evident in the fashion for
canals – long, rectangular ponds usually anchored by a pavilion at
one end. A late 17th-century example survives at Westbury Court
in Gloucestershire, painstakingly preserved by the National Trust,
and one of the most complete surviving Dutch-style water-gardens
in the country (above). However, despite their increasingly
ornamental appearance, these ponds were still very much employed
for the provision of food, as recounted by John Evelyn on a visit to
Swallowfield in Berkshire in 1685:

*Above all, The Canale, and fish ponds, the one fed with a white, the other with a
black-running water, fed by swift and quick river: so well and plentifully stor'd with fish,
that for Pike, Carp, Bream, & Tench; I had never seene any thing approaching it: we had
Carps & Pikes &c of size fit for the table of a prince, every meale, & what added to the
delight, the seeing hundreds taken in the drag, out of which the Cooke standing by, we
pointed to what we had most mind to, & had Carps every meale, that had been worth
at London twenty shill a piece.*

FISH PONDS AND LAKES

FISH FOR DINNER

Pike, carp, tench and perch were the staples of the fish ponds. In 1781 the Norfolk cleric Parson Woodforde records, 'I gave my company for Dinner my great Pike which was rosted & a Pudding in his Belly.' This refers to the traditional method of stuffing fish or other small game with a mix of cereal and fat. He proudly notes that all the company were 'quite astonished at the sight of the great Pike on the table' which was accompanied by 'some boiled Trout, Perch and Tench, Eel and Gudgeon Fryed'.

Pike

This long-lived predatory fish was sometimes kept in a separate pond on account of its cannibalistic tendencies. It is rarely eaten

The polite sport of angling was a favourite pastime of the gentry, as illustrated in this portrait of Francis Popham by Arthur Devis (1711–1787).

today, having the disadvantage of being full of bones, but it was once a dinner-party staple, with a mushroomy taste and a fine texture, tending to dryness in an older fish, which were classically used to make quenelles (a poached dumpling of minced fish and breadcrumbs), although the small fish were particularly good fried whole and served with a sauce.

Perch

This is a relatively small fish, rarely weighing more than 350g (12oz). It was found in nearly all the lakes and rivers around Britain, and bred in large numbers in fish ponds. It is considered one of the best fish with a taste and texture comparable to sea bass, having none of the muddy taste associated with other freshwater fish. It keeps well and does not fall apart when cooked. It is traditionally served with a *beurre blanc* sauce. The addition of sherry in Mrs Beeton's 19th-century recipe (see box, right) would elevate it to formal dining.

Perch Stewed with Wine

SERVES 4–6
4 perch
Equal quantities of stock and sherry
1 bayleaf
1 clove of garlic
a small bunch of parsley
2 cloves
salt to taste
thickening of butter and flour
pepper
grated nutmeg
½ teaspoon anchovy sauce

MODE – Scale the fish then take out the gills, and clean them thoroughly; lay the fish in a stewpan with sufficient stock and sherry to just cover them. Put in the bayleaf, garlic, parsley, cloves, salt, and simmer till tender. When done, take out the fish and strain the liquor, add a thickening of butter and flour, the pepper, nutmeg, and the anchovy sauce, and stir it over the fire until somewhat reduced, pour over the fish, and serve.

ISABELLA BEETON, *The Book of Household Management* (1861)

A Pike and a Perch, illustrated in the Illustrated London Almanack *(1864).*

Salmon in Pastry

SERVES 4–6
115g (4oz) butter
3 pieces preserved ginger, chopped small
2 tbsp currants
1 tbsp chopped almonds
pinch of ground mace
salt and pepper
675g (1½lb) salmon, in 2 fillets
350g (12oz) puff pastry, thinly rolled
  and chilled
1 egg, beaten

Preheat the oven to 220°C (425°F, Gas Mark 7). Mix the butter, ginger, currants, almonds and mace together and season with salt and pepper. Use half to sandwich the fillets of salmon together and put the rest on top. Brush egg on the inner face of the pastry and wrap around the salmon, sealing the edges. Score the pastry casing with a crisscross pattern. Brush with the remainder of the egg and bake in the oven for 30 minutes.

Tench

Belonging to the same family as carp, tench is often found in muddy waters and has to be thoroughly purged in clean water before eating. It was, however, esteemed as delicious and wholesome and has a soft and tasty flesh. In 1760, at Charlecote Park in Warwickshire, the housekeeper Philippa Hayes recorded in her notebook the 'fish taken out of the Great Bason in the court for the master's dinner' since her master had an appetite for freshwater fish, in particular for 'a whole tench boiled in ale and dressed with lemon and rosemary'.

Carp

This was the favourite fish during the Tudor period, superseding bream as the principal inhabitant of the fish ponds. A long-lived fish, it is ideal for farming as it grows and multiplies at a rapid rate. It feeds at the bottom of the pond and therefore, as with tench, needs to be purged of muddy water before being cooked; it has a firm, meaty flesh suitable for cooking in a variety of ways, especially baking. It featured consistently on dinner-party menus up until the 19th century. Although rarely eaten in Britain today, it remains very popular in Eastern European countries where it is traditionally served at Christmas, and it is still widely used in both Chinese and Jewish cuisine.

Fish from the rivers

As well as the fish derived from artificial ponds, many estate owners had access to well-stocked rivers that provided sport as well as food.

SALMON

Salmon is as popular today as it was 550 years ago, when the prioress and writer Dame Juliana Berners commented that 'the salmon is the most stately fish that any man can angle for in fresh water'. Wild salmon feed and mature in salt water before swimming up river to spawn, and are at their best when they arrive at the river's mouth. However, most of the salmon available today are the product of intensive fish farms. Salmon can be cooked many ways, but to take best advantage of its handsome appearance, poach it whole and serve with hollandaise sauce. Alternatively, to experience the unusual medieval style of combining sweet flavours with fish, try an adaptation of the late George Perry-Smith's deceptively simple recipe for salmon in pastry, as delicious as it is unexpected (see left).

THE "BOY'S OWN PAPER"]

GROVER & CO., NOTTINGHAM.

[56, Paternoster Row.

OUR BRITISH FRESH WATER FISH.

Drawn for the "Boy's Own Paper" by A. F. LYDON.

An assortment of freshwater fish illustrated in The Boy's Own Paper *(1896)*

Eel spearers at work on the marshes at Reculver, Kent, in the 1930s. Skilled eel catchers caught as many as 4.5kg (10lb) of eels an hour.

EELS

The life cycle of the eel remained a mystery for centuries until it was discovered in the early 1900s that they start their life in the Sargasso Sea in the Atlantic Ocean and spend their first three years swimming to the rivers of Europe to mature before returning to the sea and their spawning grounds to breed. They were once a universally popular fish and country families especially relied on them as a source of fresh fish, either fried, scrambled with egg or made into a fishy bread. Today they are rarely available other than jellied, a speciality of the east end of London. However, the area around the rivers Severn and Wye still supports an ancient eel fishery where elvers, the young of the eel (also known as glass eels) can be caught. These

RECIPE

Cooking an Eel

It is agreed by most men, that the eel is a most dainty fish ... How to make this Eel a most excellent dish of meat. First, wash him in water and salt; then pull off his skin below his vent or navel, and not much further: having done that, take out his guts as clean as you can, but wash him not: then give him three or four scotches with a knife; and then put into his belly and those scotches, sweet herbs, an anchovy, and a little nutmeg grated or cut very small; and your herbs and anchovies must also be cut very small; and mixt with good butter and salt: having done this, then pull his skin over him, all but his head, which you are to cut off, to the end you may tie his skin about that part where his head grew, and it must be so tied as to keep all his moisture within his skin: and having done this, tie him with tape or packthread to a spit, and roast him leisurely; and baste him with water and salt till his skin breaks, and then with butter; and having roasted him enough, let what was put into his belly, and what he drips, be his sauce.

IZAAK WALTON, *The Compleat Angler* (1653)

were traditionally eaten in the west of the country, and were served as a speciality in fashionable Bath. Silver eels – those caught in the autumn when ready to migrate back to the sea – are considered a delicacy, especially when smoked.

CRAYFISH

Monks in medieval Britain were very fond of crayfish and it has been suggested that they were responsible for introducing them into streams. The Victorians liked to use them as a garnish for boiled turkey or fish, or for a calf's head. They resemble small lobsters and can be cooked in the same way. However, today the native white-clawed crayfish is a protected species since its numbers have been reduced by 95 per cent following the introduction of the larger and aggressive American signal crayfish during the 1990s.

The native British crayfish is threatened by pollution and the recently introduced American signal crayfish.

*One of a collection of stuffed
fish in a glass case on the
staircase and landing at
Overbeck's, Devon.*

Preserved fish

Since fish perishes quickly once killed, preserving it by salting,
smoking, pickling or drying was done to extend its shelf life.
Sea fish such as cod were dried and known as stockfish, while
herrings were salted at sea before they were landed. Pickling was an
alternative method of preserving fish: portions of salmon, sturgeon,
pike and eels were rolled up and soused in vinegar, wine or beer,
just as roll-mops, or pickled herring, are sold today. Some fish were
fried prior to being pickled in vinegar, known as 'caveached', to be
served as a side dish, while potted fish was a fashionable and useful
method of preserving where the ingredients were sealed in a pot
under a layer of melted butter. Suitable fish included eels, salmon,
lampreys, smelts, mackerel, lobsters, crabs and shrimps.

One of the most widely used fish, the anchovy, was not from
our shores at all, but from the Mediterranean. It had long been
enjoyed pickled, and by the end of the 17th century was used as a
garum, a fermented fish sauce which eventually evolved into a 'new
sawce called a catch-up, from East India' to be used as a seasoning
in an infinite number of fish, meat and salad recipes. It is included
in both Izaak Walton's eel recipe (see page 122) and Mrs Beeton's
perch recipe (see page 119).

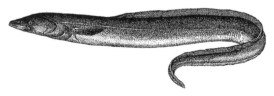

KITCHEN GARDEN ESTATE

ANGLING

The provision of fish may have been the main purpose of early ponds, but the potential for sports such as fishing and sailing was soon exploited as an additional bonus. Scenes of families enjoying a day's fishing are a constant theme in paintings throughout the 18th and 19th centuries. Early examples are usually set within the safe confines of the estate, as shown in *Fishing Party* by Edward Smith (1773), in which a mixed group are enjoying various activities in the garden, including angling, with a female member of the party holding up her catch (right). In *The Fishing Party* by Joseph Farrington and John Hoppner (c.1803), the participants have ventured into the wilder rivers in the landscape beyond, reflecting an increasing interest in the natural world.

Angling was enjoyed by the whole family, as depicted in this conversation piece, **Fishing Party (1773)** *by Edward Smith.*

The most famous name in the history of angling must surely be that of Izaak Walton who, in *The Compleat Angler* (1653), described the sport as 'the contemplative man's recreation'. The book contains a diverse mix of factual information, dialogue and songs, including this folk song affirming the pleasures of angling:

Man's life is but vain, for 'tis subject to pain
And sorrow, and short as a bubble:
'Tis hodge-podge of business and money and care
And care and money and trouble

But we'll take no care when the weather proves fair,
Nor will we now vex though it rain;
We'll banish all sorrow, and sing till to-morrow
And angle and angle again

These sentiments are reinforced by Roger North, who derived much pleasure from fishing, with both rods and nets. Exaggerated stories of the size of a catch are clearly nothing new:

Young people love Angling extremely: then there is a Boat, which gives Pleasure enough in Summer, frequent fishing with Nets, the very making of Nets, seeing the Waters, much Discussion of them, and the Fish, especially upon your great Sweeps, and the strange Surprises that will happen in Numbers and Bigness.

Whether in rivers or ponds, angling combined the traditional bedfellows of pleasure and usefulness; it was a popular contemplative pastime, part of rural life and country retirement. Parson Woodforde enjoyed a successful afternoon fishing, being particularly taken with a fish called a Cruzer, as he records in his diary entry of April 1778:

Sailing boats and, in the foreground, fishermen and drag nets, animate this river scene of **Windsor Castle** *by William Marlow (1740–1813).*

'*We spent the forenoon a fishing in Mr Howes's pond — I lent him my large drag Net, and my Cart carried it over for him … We caught vast Quantities of Fish, called Cruzers, they are a very beautiful Fish of a yellow hue but not very large, almost all the same size — some few small Carp & Tench. I gave Mr Howes 20 brace of stock Tench, and he gave me in return 50 brace of Cruzers.*'

This gives an indication of the large quantities of fish that would have been stocked in the pond. Mr Howe was certainly very generous with his cruzers, identified as crucian carp, a very attractive little fish just as the parson described. Its origins are uncertain, but it was possibly introduced to this country in the 18th century to embellish the newly created ornamental lakes of the landscape parks. This did not prevent the Parson eating one fried for his supper which he considered 'very good indeed'.

Exchanging fish with friends or offering your lake or river for others to enjoy was a customary gesture; in Jane Austin's *Pride and Prejudice* (1813), Mr Darcy encounters Elizabeth Bennet and her aunt and uncle walking along the river in his park at Pemberley:

The conversation soon turned upon fishing, and she heard Mr Darcy invite him, with the greatest civility, to fish there as often as he chose … offering at the same time to supply him with fishing tackle, and pointing out those parts of the stream where there was usually most sport.

River fishing was increasingly popular as people were venturing further into the open countryside for their sport. In May 1778 Parson Woodforde went to Lenwade Bridge in Norfolk to fish in the river where he caught 'a prodigious fine Pike which weighed 8 pounds and a half and had in its Belly another Pike of above a Pound – we also caught there the finest Trout I ever saw which weighed 3 Pounds and ten ounces'.

Essential tools for the keen fisherman comprising a rod, reels, a box of flies and haversack.

As the Parson discovered with his catch, pike were known to be a cannibal breed. Ben Johnson's celebration of the fish ponds at Penshurst in Kent (1612) captures the various characteristics of fish, not only of pike but in this passage also the slothful carp and slippery eels:

And if the high-swollen Medway fail thy dish,
Thou hast thy ponds that pay thee tribute fish:
Fat, aged carps, that run unto thy net;
And pikes, now weary their own kind to eat,
As loth the second cast or draught to stay,
Officiously at first themselves betray;
Bright eels, that emulate them and leap on land
Before the fisher, or into his hand.'

THE BEGINNING OF DECLINE

Although fish ponds continued to be built well into the 19th century in provincial estates, they began a gradual decline in popularity from 1600. John Taverner, author of *Certaine Experiments concerning Fishe and Fruit* (1600), records that fish ponds had once been more popular in England but that many of his contemporaries preferred to keep chickens and rabbits, with fish being transferred from the artificial ponds into rivers. The increasing popularity of river fishing, together with the ill effects of stagnant water, may have contributed to the demise of fish ponds. Technology for fountains and water-powered automata began to appear, influenced by the Renaissance gardens in Italy. Moving water had none of the disadvantages of a still pool. Francis Bacon, in his essay *Of Gardens* (c.1625),

The ornamental values of the 18th century are clear in the architectural embellishments that adorned the water gardens at Studley Royal, Yorkshire. Balthasar Nebot's painting (c.1768) looks south towards the Cascade and fishing tabernacles with the Octagon Tower to the left and the Banqueting House on the right.

wrote of how he disliked stagnant water, maintaining 'pools mar all, and make the garden unwholesome and full of flies and frogs', whereas fountains 'are a great beauty and refreshment'.

This was reinforced over a century later in John James's *The Theory and Practice of Gardening* (1707), in which he champions the fashion for formal French-style gardens and dismisses stagnant water as 'the most disagreeable of all; it grows dirty, green, and all covered with Moss and Filth, having no Motion at all, as in Basons that seldom play, and in marshy Lakes and Ponds: They are also very subject to corrupt, and to stink, in the Summer.' This dislike of ponds may in part be due to a failure to keep the strict management regime imposed on the medieval fish ponds, which were drained and cleaned on a regular basis.

By the 18th century the ornamental value of water and its potential use for sailing and angling was beginning to supersede its function as a larder, which resulted in the transformation of many fish ponds into ornamental lakes. The changing perception of water in the garden from formal pond to naturalistic pool is implied in a letter from Mrs Elizabeth Robinson to her daughter Elizabeth Montague in 1743:

'He wants some better name than that of a pond for his water which puzzles him very much for he fears it is too small to call a Serpentine river, but thinks that of a pool wou'd sound [better] than a pond, your father proposes that he should call it ye temple Pool or Sacred pool.'

Lakes were constructed for practical as well as aesthetic reasons. At Croome Park in Worcestershire, Lancelot 'Capability' Brown transformed what was a boggy 'morass' by digging a lake into which the surplus water could be drained, thereby creating a reservoir of water for household use (below). However, most apparent was the quality that a naturalistic stretch of water lent to the evolving landscape park, summed up by Thomas Whatley who, in 1770, described Brown's lake at Wotton House in Buckinghamshire where the mildness of character is 'still more forcibly felt when the shadows grow feint as they lengthen: when a little rustling of birds in the spray, the leaping of the fish, and the fragrancy of the woodbine, denote the approach of evening'.

The lake offering rippled reflections of the house at Croome Park, Worcestershire.

Architectural ornament

In the 18th century these newly created lakes were designed for enjoyment rather than just to look at. Pavilions and fishing houses were sited along their banks to serve as venues for the various pleasures on offer. One of the prettiest surviving fishing pavilions, designed in 1769 by Robert Adam, the most fashionable architect of his day, can be found by the water's edge at Kedleston Hall in Derbyshire (below). It was originally flanked by weeping willows and waterside shrubs to provide a screen from the prying eyes of the main house, thus reinforcing a feeling of seclusion and intimacy. Inside a little banqueting room overlooking the lake is a tall window from which to cast your fishing line. The walls are decorated with seascapes (right) and a classical statue of Venus surveys the whole proceedings. The fireplace would have ensured plenty of warmth for drying off after a dip in the cold bath downstairs or returning from a turn on the lake in a rowing boat from the adjoining boathouse. However, while the pavilion was designed to have many functions, it was equally important as an architectural focal point amid the naturalistic lines of the park.

Robert Adam's Fishing Pavilion at Kedleston Hall, Derbyshire, was designed in 1769 and built in 1770–2 so that the Curzons could fish from the upper window protected from both sun and rain.

The lake became the aquatic equivalent of the deer park, providing both sport and food for the household. This was recognised by Humphrey Repton in his Red Book for Holkham Hall in Norfolk in which he recommends a dwelling for the 'water porter' which might 'resemble some fishing huts on the banks of the Severn … the man shou'd have the care of the boats … and be at hand to navigate the pleasure boats when any lady may require it … he will become a sort of aquatic gamekeeper; and his house a kind of water Porter's Lodge'.

At about the same time that Humphrey Repton was making improvements to gardens across the country, John Plaw's book *Ferme Ornée* (1795) offered designs for ornamental farm buildings in which he echoes Repton's suggestion for a water porter; his design for a fishing lodge contained 'accommodations for Tea-drinking parties, Fishing tackle' in the front and to the rear 'accommodations for a Keeper, who would have the care of the waters and the fishery, and his family'.

FISHING TODAY

Today, the lakes and ponds of private gardens are now usually maintained for purely ornamental purposes; the colonies of carp that may lurk therein are cursed for muddying the clear waters rather than celebrated at the dining table. Ironically for an island nation, our former appreciation of fish has become limited to the national dish of battered fish and chips. With concerning issues of sustainability threatening the sea-fishing industry, a few stalwarts in the restaurant industry are rediscovering the lost flavours from our rivers, ponds and lakes. Perhaps by revisiting the past we can reignite our love of this country's freshwater produce and once again enjoy the combined benefits of sport, food and beauty that fish ponds can sustainably offer.

Two of the fish paintings, **Atlantic Salmon and Allis Shad By the River Wye** *(left) and* **Flounders and Smelts** *(right), by Arthur Devis (c.1772) that adorn the interior of the Fishing Pavilion at Kedleston Hall, Derbyshire.*

Dovecotes and Poultry Yards

'Among the orchard weeds, from every search,
Snugly and sure, the old hen's nest is made,
Who cackles every morning from her perch
To tell the servant girl new eggs are laid.'

— JOHN CLARE, *Hen's Nest* (1793–1864)

Doves in flight around the roof
of the octagonal dovecote in
the walled garden at Felbrigg
Hall, Norfolk.

Dovecotes and poultry yards were among the most profitable features of the historic estate. Nothing was wasted because just about every part of the bird, including its dung, could be used; the eggs were a versatile ingredient in the kitchen, while the flesh was a welcome source of protein, especially during the lean winter months when other meat was scarce. The feathers had a multitude of uses. They filled pillows and beds (the superstitious believed that sleeping on pigeon feathers ensured a long life), were transformed into quills for writing or for fishing flies and for fletching arrows to ensure a straight line of flight, and the finest of all adorned hats and costumes.

The dung proved equally versatile, not only as a highly effective fertiliser, but also in the tanning industry for softening the leather, and in the manufacture of saltpetre in the production of gunpowder. In addition, the more exotic species of bird were valued as an ornamental asset as they strutted around the garden and park. For sport, pigeons were offered up for hawking and shooting competitions, while cockerels were sacrificed to the blood-thirsty entertainment of cock fighting.

The dovecote at Nymans, West Sussex.

A considerable advantage of owning poultry was that it involved little financial outlay, and thus was within the means of cottagers and country landowners alike. While owning a dovecote in the Middle Ages was restricted to the nobility and the monasteries, most rural cottage gardens would have had a few hens scratching about the yard. The parks of the greater estates were adorned with more ornamental birds such as swans and peacocks, also destined for the banqueting table.

The agricultural improvements of the 18th century ensured that a wider variety of meat was available all year round and so the reliance on pigeon meat in winter was reduced. However, pigeon numbers remained high and they eventually took up residence in our burgeoning towns and cities. Those that did not turn feral found a new role in the emerging sport of pigeon racing, adopted with enthusiasm by the working classes in northern England. By contrast, the poultry yard became ever more popular and collecting and rearing the pretty hens was considered a suitable pastime for the lady of the house. Despite the mass production of eggs and chickens in the 19th and 20th centuries, keeping hens has remained an enjoyable and profitable pastime for both town and country dwellers to this day.

DOVECOTES

An interior view of the dovecote on the second floor of the south-west turret at Tattershall Castle, Lincolnshire.

Although no longer used to rear meat, dovecotes can still be found in the grounds of manor houses and monasteries; inside, a chequered pattern of nesting boxes reveals the purpose of these ancient buildings. A single dovecote could contain anything from a few hundred to a few thousand birds, depending on its size. As there is little meat on each bird, this accounts for the great quantity required for the extensive noble households. The pigeons housed within were descendants of the blue rock pigeon (*Columba livia*) better suited to domestication than the smaller wild wood pigeon.

During the Middle Ages dovecotes, being limited to the nobility and the church, became associated with status and wealth, although they were unpopular with neighbouring farmers whose crops were ravaged by the birds. There was a preference for positioning the dovecote close to the main house for security from robbers and protection from predators. The Norfolk landowner Roger North advised in his treatise *On Building* (c.1695) that the dovecote be close to the Hall in order to protect the pigeons from hawks: 'Woodlands harbour Hawkes, the desperate enimys of these poor birds that inhabit with us. And it is for that reason not to pitch the house too far from company.' Moreover, such a prominent location would reinforce the structure's importance as a status symbol. The ideal situation was away from trees and sheltered from the prevailing wind. Access to water was essential and an example of siting dovecotes near the estate fish ponds can be seen at Cotehele in Cornwall, where the circular, domed dovecote is situated close to the stew pond.

The laws restricting ownership of a dovecote were relaxed by 1600 and by the end of the 17th century their numbers increased to such an extent that it was estimated there were as many 26,000 in the land. Their numbers declined with the advent of agricultural improvements in the 18th century that enabled cattle to be fed throughout the winter, thereby ensuring year-round availability of meat. Today only a fraction of that number remains, redundant of their original purpose but some restored as a reminder of our architectural and agricultural heritage.

Architectural styles

A traditional dovecote is a one-room structure with walls 1m (3¼ft) thick or more, lined inside with rows of nesting-boxes. Some still contain their original 'potence', a device made up of a central rotating wooden pole with arms to which a ladder was attached and used for collecting the eggs or the squabs, young birds culled at about four weeks old as these provided the sweetest, most tender meat. Pigeons accessed the buildings via an entrance through the roof, which was usually topped with a cupola to prevent rain entering, or they would fly in through a side opening high up in the walls or gables.

Early dovecotes tended to be circular; the dovecote at Dunster Castle in Somerset is believed to have been built at the time of William the Conqueror, with later alterations. It stands about 5.8m (19ft) high and the same in diameter and still has a working potence. Antony in Cornwall has the rare distinction of having two dovecotes, a very large brick circular one that stands behind the house and still contains pigeons (below) and a much older ruined dovecote in the nearby woods. Dovecotes in the form of circular towers were possibly adapted from the remains of earlier fortified buildings; at

The 18th-century dovecote in the gardens at Antony, Cornwall.

Bodiam Castle in East Sussex one of the towers served as a dovecote, discernible only by the nesting boxes inside.

Dovecotes could also be square, or less commonly rectangular and divided in the middle to form in effect two pigeon-houses – perhaps a way of getting around the law permitting only one dovecote for each property. Inside the 16th-century rectangular dovecote at Geddington in Northampton, each of the two compartments could house a thousand pairs of birds. Another impressive dovecote built around the same time at Willington in Bedfordshire and of a similar formation is distinguished by its crow-stepped gables, a rarity south of the Scottish border.

The material used to build the dovecote depended on the locality. Cob, a mixture of mud and straw, was popular in the West Country; flint was used in the eastern counties, while the Cotswolds favoured honey-coloured limestone. The attractive black-and-white timber-framed building style typical of Herefordshire and Worcestershire can be appreciated in two fine 17th-century dovecotes at Hawford Grange and at Wichenford Court, both in Worcestershire and owned and carefully restored by the National Trust. By the 17th and 18th centuries dovecotes were built not only for practical purposes but as an ornament to the garden. These new models, often octagonal or hexagonal in shape, were commonly built of brick, which lent itself to surface pattern, especially when combined with contrasting materials such as flint. Felbrigg Hall in Norfolk has a fine example from 1750, built into the kitchen garden wall (left).

As large-scale pigeon production waned it became more practical to combine dovecotes with other estate buildings. At Downhill, Co. Londonderry, the dovecote forms the upper half of the ice house, and at Calke Abbey in Derbyshire and Belton House in Lincolnshire the dovecotes form the second storey of the stables. Nesting boxes were also built into the gables or lofts of houses and barns.

The octagonal brick dovecote at Felbrigg Hall, Norfolk, with the kitchen garden wall flanking either side.

Pigeon pye

Favourite dishes were pigeon dumplings and a 'Grand Patty of Pidgeons Royal'. The birds were generally eaten as squabs. Despite the gradual decline in dovecote numbers, pigeon remained a very popular dish well into the 18th and 19th centuries. Viscount Torrington, on his travels around the country in the 1780s, enjoyed nothing more than ending the day with a meal of 'port wine and Pigeons'. On one occasion such was his enjoyment of an 'excellent pigeon pye' he was inspired to compose the following verse in its praise:

> Pri'thee tell me, what can vie,
> Or eat like a pigeon pye;
> Nought so pleasing to the eye,
> As charming as pigeon pye;
> If my appetite is high,
> What's so good as pigeon pye,
> Ever let me till I die,
> Taste the charms of pigeon pye;
> That you may not think I lye,
> Ask a well made pigeon pye.

Fancy pigeon breeds by A.F. Lydon in **The Boy's Own** *paper of the late 19th century.*

Certainly what the Viscount lacked in talent for poetry he more than made up for in his enthusiasm for the subject.

Since the 20th century domestic pigeon has all but disappeared from the menu in favour of its wild woodland cousin, rendering dovecotes redundant, with ruinous consequences. The inhabitant pigeons have turned feral to scavenge the cities and towns. Any remaining dovecotes stand as charming follies, still housing flocks of pigeons but no longer taken for food. Small wooden dovecotes sold today as garden ornaments are a nod to past privileges but with no intention of serving the tenant birds for supper. Yet the meat of the young bird is lean and easily digestible with high levels of minerals and vitamins and the population of birds is such that there would be a plentiful supply of this free-range meat if the appetite for this once highly valued bird was regained.

FEASTS AND FEATHERS

From the Middle Ages swans and peacocks were eaten as part of a banquet until they were usurped in favour of the newer arrivals from abroad; guinea fowl had been introduced to Britain from West Africa in the 16th century around the same time as the turkey, which originated in the Americas and was fast becoming the favourite bird for celebrations and feasts. Swans were retained mainly for their stateliness, but continued to be enjoyed on special occasions well into the 18th century. Samuel Pepys' diary for 14 January 1666 records 'At noon ate the second of the two cygnets Mr Shepley sent us for a New Year's gift', and as late as 1750 William Ellis, in *The Country Housewife's Family Companion*, described fattened cygnets as a 'dainty Dish'.

Male peacock in the gardens of Powis Castle, Powys. After their decline on the banqueting table, peacocks retained their value as the most glamorous of birds to adorn the garden.

Before they were consumed at the table, these flamboyant beauties had another role to play in the parks and gardens of the country houses. Swans, peacocks and myriad other ornamental birds were allowed to swagger around the grounds, providing glamour and animation. In a 1729 engraving of the celebrated Orange Tree Garden at Chiswick House, London, exotic peacocks roam freely around the terraces of equally exotic orange trees, while a painting by Nicholas Dall of the artificial ruins at Shugborough Hall in Staffordshire dating from 1775 depicts a trio of peacocks pecking the lawn where the gardeners have just swept, with a group of swans and cygnets gliding on the serpentine lake in the distance. In a diary entry of 1787, Viscount Torrington describes the 'Modern Taste', for which he had a notorious disdain. He takes a satirical view on scenes such as these, giving a tongue-in-cheek recommendation to 'Keep numbers of peacocks and Guinea fowls, who will make delightful serenades, added to the cheerful sounds of the geese and the poultry; but this is all in the way of rural propriety and simplicity.'

POULTRY

Unlike pigeons, which were restricted to monasteries and manor houses, hens, ducks and geese were kept in small cottages and large estates alike. Most poultry would have been contained within a yard or coop to protect the garden from the pecking and scratching habits of fowl. In a detail from a late 17th-century painting of Badminton House in Gloucestershire, a series of poultry yards are shown in close proximity to the house. One yard holds silver and gold birds, probably pheasants, while the next one is home to a pair of exotic ostriches, whose feathers were a heraldic symbol of power, and a larger enclosure to the right contains a dovecote (above). The yards in the foreground are the kitchen gardens, with vegetable beds and fruit trained on the walls, and to the left is the piggery, all within easy access of the kitchen.

Late 17th-century painting of Badminton House, Gloucestershire, showing all the necessary components of the self-sufficient estate, including the dovecote and poultry yards with exotic birds situated around the house.

Palatial poultry yards

Tending the delicate birds in the poultry yard was deemed
a suitable pastime for ladies. The mistress of the house would have
responsibility for the overall management, and in well-staffed
households the dairy-maid would take on the day-to-day duties,
thus perpetuating the idealised image of pastoral life captured
in a 19th-century illustration of a young woman feeding hens
in front of a picturesque thatched cottage (below).

At Croome Park in Worcestershire, Lady Coventry was a major
force in creating the celebrated late 18th-century park laid out by
Lancelot 'Capability' Brown. The horticultural collection alone was
described by a contemporary as 'second only to Kew'. Proving that
she had commercial instincts, she established a menagerie in 1768

*The feminine duties of
the poultry yard are
captured in this idealised
19th-century illustration.*

which contained exotic poultry such as silver pheasants, Canada and Cape geese, Turkish ducks, white turkeys, guinea fowl, and the exotic 'Sparrows of Paradise', a pair of red-headed parakeets, a 'Nunn' bird and a 'Snow bird'. Such was the success of Lady Coventry's menagerie that by 1780 the architect Robert Adam, who was working on several buildings at Croome at the time, was employed to enhance it by adding a banqueting house with adjoining tea-room. The scheme also included a keeper's house, for, although Lady Coventry initially supervised the management of the birds herself, her success was such that she found it necessary to employ a keeper by the name of Mr Watmoug. Although, as with many grand schemes, the plans were never fully realised, they remain an indication of the status of Lady Coventry's feathered collection.

Improved husbandry was a growing concern from the late 18th century. Sir John Soane's designs for the poultry houses at Wimpole Hall in Cambridgeshire combined an ornate building with a prime concern for the welfare of the inhabitants. His drawings show a symmetrical classical composition of timber boxes with arched openings and nests. Sadly these buildings do not exist at Wimpole today and, as with Adam's plans for Croome, it is possible they

Windsor Home Park: the Aviary and Poultry Farm (1845) by Caleb Robert Stanley. Prince Albert brought ornamental birds with him to England in 1840 and his aviary at Windsor accommodated varieties of poultry, doves, bustards, storks and pheasants.

were never actually built. Nevertheless, the employment of one of the leading architects of the day to design an agricultural building with the same architectural vocabulary as the family house is an indication of the high importance the country gentleman placed on his rural estate.

One of the finest examples of a poultry house, or aviary as it was called, was built for Queen Victoria and Prince Albert in the home farm at Windsor Castle in 1845. Prince Albert had fond recollections of the aviaries enjoyed during his childhood in Germany, and after his marriage he introduced a large number of birds of many varieties to both Buckingham Palace and Windsor. Although highly ornamental, the aviary was nevertheless designed to be perfectly adapted to the needs of the birds (see page 141). It consisted of a pavilion flanked by roosting boxes and breeding and laying nests, made to resemble as closely as possible those which the birds would form in a natural state. At the top was an elegant dovecote lined with mirrors where, it was noted, 'pigeons delight to gaze while they prune and dress their feathers'. The Queen was a frequent visitor and even had her own sitting room there. In August 1858 she 'inspected the charming brood of wee little bantams' and commented that 'nothing could be cleaner or better kept, all the hen coops or pigeon coops done with moss and heather'. The poultry breeds included Cochin China, Black Spanish, Dorking, Hamburg, Andalusian and Poland breeds, together with bantams, peacocks, turkeys, geese, doves and even storks. Sadly, at the end of Victoria's reign, the poultry was dispersed and buildings at the home farm were converted into domestic accommodation.

For the middle classes such expense would have been prohibitive and inappropriate. In her *Ladies' Country Companion* (1845), Jane Loudon caters for 'ladies who have been brought up in town, but who from circumstances have been induced to reside in the country'. She provides detailed instructions on creating the ideal poultry yard and confirms that the 'duties of attending poultry are completely feminine'. The poultry yards, she recommends, should be at least half an acre (0.2ha) – still a sizeable area – with a hen house at one end and a pond at the other, with a tree in the middle for roosting pea and guinea fowl. The yard should be half laid down to gravel, the other half grass. Along with hens and turkeys, ducks and geese could be housed in the poultry yard but should be at the pond end, with guinea fowl roosting in the trees. Loudon advises that peacocks should not be kept in the poultry yard as they 'have a propensity for killing all young fowls they can reach'.

*'Hen and Chickens' (c.1905),
a nursery frieze published by
Lawrence and Jellicoe.*

Farmers and cottagers

A more economical alternative to a poultry yard was to utilise
an existing loft, perhaps above a pigsty or other livestock barn,
which would provide warmth to encourage egg-laying in the
colder months. Access for collecting eggs and cleaning the coop
was through a small door and hens could get in and out through
a pop-hole, although by the 18th century it was not uncommon
for hens to be shut inside all the time.

Common varieties of hen would have been kept in these more
modest dwellings. Pure-bred exotic fowl such as those found in
Lady Coventry's menagerie and Queen Victoria's aviary were the
domain of the wealthy landowning classes, although their cockerels
were put 'out to walk' with farmers' poultry, resulting in crossbred
birds. These 'dunghill hens' provided enough eggs and meat for the
immediate household and a few spare to sell for pin money, which
would have supplemented the household income. As William Ellis
explains in his *Country Housewife's Family Companion* (1750) 'Poultry and
their eggs come more immediately under the Care and Management
of our Country Housewife, than any other outward Part of the
Farmer's Business.' It was with the profit from selling the eggs
and chicken that she was able to buy the 'trivial Necessaries in
the House, as Sugar, Plumbs, Spices, Salt, Oatmeal Etc.'

For the country housewife the temperament and conformation
of the hen were sensibly more important than a flamboyant
appearance. The ideal characteristics were pointed out by
Gervase Markham in about 1600.

*Your Hen must be perfectly bred as your Cooke ... and her head would be smal, her eye
very cheerfull and her Crowne armed with a double Cof(s)pel or Crownet; her body
would be large, for so shee will cover her Broode the better, and the feathers on her brest*

would be long and downie, for that is most comfort to the Chickens … if she has no spurres it is better for her Broode and no impeachment to her Valure. Lastly looke that she be a painfulle layer, a willing Sitter; and above all things loving and kinde to her Broode. If your Hen chance to Crow, which is an evill and unnatural infirmity to her, you shall forthwith pull her wings and give her wheat scorched and mixt with powder of Chaulke and keepe her … from the companie of all other pulline.

This harsh recommendation is a reminder of some of the less attractive aspects of the husbandry involved in rearing poultry. Geese were plucked up to five times a year, the best feathers coming from live birds. Cockerels not required for breeding were castrated at about six weeks old and it fell to the housewife to perform the procedure. These birds were subsequently known as capons which grew fat and were available for the pot in spring, when the laying hens were retained for egg production. An early recipe from the 14th century, cited in Dorothy Hartley's *Food in England*, regards capon favourably:

Of all tame fowls a capon is moste bests for it is nutytyne and soon dyggestyd — A Henne in winter is good and so is a chyken in somer especyallye cockrellys and polettes … The fleshs of a cocke is harde of dygestyon but the broth or gely made of a cocke is restorative.

Force-feeding poultry was commonplace, a practice still performed in parts of the world today, most notably in France for the production of the luxury *foie gras*. Sir Kenelm Digby records in his notebook of 1669 the effects of overfeeding chickens on crushed raisins, white breadcrumbs and milk, so that 'the delight of this meat will make them eat continually and they will be so fat (when they are but the bigness of a blackbird) that they will not be able to stand, but lie down upon their bellies to eat'. The fatter they were the more profit made.

Cockerel in the gardens at Godolphin House, Cornwall.

KITCHEN GARDEN ESTATE

Eggs

Originally, hens were valued primarily for their eggs – a versatile and valuable part of the diet across the social spectrum. Hens would have been culled for eating only when their prime egg-laying days were over. From the Middle Ages eggs were consumed on their own, often poached and sometimes fried. Eggs were not commonly eaten boiled before the 16th century, but were baked in the soft ash of the wood fire. They were rarely eaten more than one or two at a time, the opinion being that 'one egg is gentility, two sufficient and more excess'. The tradition of eggs for breakfast originated with the Victorians: clusters of boiled eggs were produced for the breakfast table along with kidneys, bacon or kedgeree. Beautifully modelled china hens covering a shallow dish filled with hot water would keep the eggs warm on the breakfast table.

Eggs were also an essential ingredient for cakes and custards. Dorothy Hartley, in *Food in England* (1954) revives an unusual old recipe from Worcestershire called Marigold Eggs (below) in which apples are cooked in pastry with a herb and marigold petal custard. This would be served with roast pork in the same way Yorkshire pudding is served with roast beef today.

Eggs became a popular breakfast for the Victorians, along with kidneys and bacon.

Marigold Eggs

Line a shallow dish with thin shortcrust pastry, butter the bottom and cover it with thinly sliced apples, and set it to bake until the apples are just cooked. Make a custard mixture of eggs beaten in milk, season strongly with pepper, salt and thyme, and a very little chopped sage, and a lot of marigold petals. Pour this savoury custard over the cooked apples and return it to the oven to bake till set.

DOROTHY HARTLEY, *Food in England* (1954)

Poultry for the table

Throughout the centuries until the present day, chicken has been consistently served as a popular and wholesome dish. Unlike wild game, which was hung for several days to tenderise the meat and improve the flavour, domestic fowl was always eaten fresh.

By the Georgian period chicken meat was elevated to a delicacy and birds were reared specifically for the table. They were cooked in many ways, most frequently boiled, roasted, or in a pie. Cold chicken might be served at picnics and buffets. Roast goose and turkey were also on the dinner menu. Parson Woodforde recorded in his late 18th-century diaries a turkey weighing 6kg (14lb) which was 'the finest fattest turkey that I ever saw, it was 2 inches [5cm] in fat on the breast after it was roasted'. This must have ensured very succulent meat, unlike many of the turkeys bred today with very little fat at all.

Roast goose had been a favourite with the Elizabethans, when it was traditionally accompanied by sorrel sauce, and it remained popular well into the 19th century. Michaelmas

19th-century painting, **Plucking the Pigeon** *by Leon Reding.*

Cockaleekie

The oldest cock is the best for Cockaleekie. Pluck, draw, but do not truss the cock, and lay him at the bottom of a well-greased iron pot. Pack around him leeks [cut into pieces], add pepper, salt, and a double handful of barley. Cover with about five quarts [5.6 litres] of water and let it simmer and simmer and simmer – and then simmer, till the bird is rag and the leeks are pulp, and the broth is lovely.

DOROTHY HARTLEY, *Food in England* (1954)

goose was fattened on the stubble fields after the harvest and commonly served with rabbit, which had also fed on the fields at the same time. The following recipe for Goose Roast with Rabbit recounted by Dorothy Hartley is an example of making the most of what was available while considering the best use for each ingredient. It has a humble provenance from a farm labourer's wife but no doubt tasted as good as a feast:

They used to pack the legs of a couple of rabbits into the goose, among the sage an onion stuffing, with slices of bacon. The rather dry rabbit meat absorbed the flavour of the goose and stuffing, and smaller children got the 'inside pieces' for their serving, as it was not so rich, and left more goose for the hungry men.

Nothing would have been wasted – even a tough old cockerel past his best would have been used for the traditional Scottish soup Cockaleekie, glorified in a verse by the comic 19th-century poet Richard Barham:

Now just such a mess of delicious hot pottage
Was smoking away when we enter'd the cottage
And casting a truly delicious perfume
Through the whole of an ugly, old, ill-furnished room.
... Poor Blogg when seeing the reeky
Repast placed before him, scarce able to speak, he
In ecstasy mutter'd, 'By Jove, Cockaleekie'!

GAME & POULTRY.

1.—Snipe on Toast.   2.—Larks on Toast.   3.—Roast Pheasant.   4.—Roast Pigeons.
5.—Roast Fowl.   6.—Roast Goose.   7.—Roast Duck.   8.—Boiled Fowl.
9.—Roast Turkey.

Game and poultry illustrated in Mrs Beeton's Household Management, *(1907) showing snipe on toast, larks, roast pheasant, pigeons, roast fowl, roast goose, roast duck, boiled fowl and roast turkey.*

KITCHEN GARDEN ESTATE

Poultry-keeping today

Recently there has been a resurgence in hen-keeping, perhaps a backlash against the intensive conditions in which many hens are farmed for commercial production, together with a realisation that keeping a few chickens at home is one of the least troublesome ways of producing your own food.

The benefits of keeping poultry today are the same as in the past: the freshest eggs, pretty feathered birds animating the garden and the quirky feature of a hen-house with all its ornamental possibilities. Hens are relatively cheap to maintain, do not require much room and, should it be your inclination, provide a chicken for the pot on their demise.

Anyone with a garden should be able to keep at least two or three hens which will provide sufficient eggs for a small family (hens prefer company so it is not advisable to keep them on their own). All that is needed is a coop, a run, and a supply of fresh water and food. Most hens are fed layers pellets or mash with some corn thrown in as a treat. Kitchen scraps are welcome too, especially salad leaves, and dairy produce such as a bit of cheese or yoghurt seems to improve the quality of the yolks. As with all livestock they are susceptible to a few ailments such as mites and worms, but good husbandry ought to keep these to a minimum. Hens should have free range of at least part of the garden during the day and be safely shut in their coop at night to protect them from foxes. They are best kept out of the vegetable garden, as they will eat as many young shoots and tasty leaves as they can find. However, their droppings make a powerful fertiliser.

It is not necessary to have a cockerel unless you are planning to breed from your hens; hens will lay eggs with or without one. Although the male of the species is more glamorous than the females he is a noisy bird, so bear this in mind if you have close neighbours. Alternatively, if you have access to an incubator, you can buy fertilised eggs to hatch at home, although there is a risk of ending up with several cockerels, which are difficult to re-home. Purchasing day-old chicks is another option if you do not mind waiting about sixteen weeks for them to begin laying eggs. However, many breeds are difficult to sex at such a young age. The simplest solution is buy point-of-lay birds, or pullets, which will provide you with eggs almost immediately. While hens can live to five or six years old, they will be at their most productive in their first two years.

Opposite: Hen with chicks on Brownsea Island, Dorset.

Breeds

There are hens to suit all levels of interest. Pure-bred hens and bantams will appeal to those who have a broad interest, perhaps wanting to exhibit their hens, or who simply take delight in their many forms. You may have to search out suppliers of particular breeds. The commercial hybrids tend to be the most prolific egg-layers and would suit those simply wanting a supply of eggs to feed a family. Most have been developed for maximum egg production while some are bred for the table; several breeds are dual-purpose. Hybrids tend to be less expensive to buy and more widely available than pure breeds. They come in a variety of colours, as do their eggs, with a choice of white, browns, pale blues and olive greens. Like their pure-bred cousins, hybrids can also be beautifully marked with cuckoo- or partridge-patterned plumage.

THREE BRITISH PURE-BREEDS

BUFF ORPINGTON *Famously the late Queen Mother's favourite breed of hen, these are large, stately, dual-purpose birds that have black, white or grey feathers or the golden buff colour from which their name is derived. They have a gentle and friendly temperament, making them ideal pets, and can lay over 150 eggs a year.*

SUSSEX *This was an important breed in the past, bred as both a table bird and for eggs, laying up to 260 cream eggs in a year. It comes in a range of colours, most commonly white with black-laced neck feathers and a black tail. The Sussex has a gentle temperament, making it ideal for beginners.*

SCOTS DUMPY *This is one of the most ancient breeds in the country and now one of the rarest. As the name suggests, it is a heavy, short-legged breed with a distinct waddle to the walk and comes in a range of colours from white, brown, gold, silver and black or the beautiful cuckoo plumage. It lays white eggs, once the most common colour of commercially produced egg but now hard to find.*

THREE HYBRID BIRDS

BLACK ROCK *A cross between a Rhode Island Red and a Plymouth Rock, this hen has glossy black and brown feathers and is a prolific layer of pale brown eggs, up to 300 in a year.*

SPECKLEDY *This cross between a Maran and a Rhode Island Red lays up to 250 dark brown eggs in a year. It is a most attractive bird, with, as the name suggests, black and white speckled feathers.*

COTSWOLD LEGBAR *If it is blue eggs you are after, this is the bird for you. A recent hybrid developed from the Cream Legbar and Araucana hen, it is prettily marked with a distinguishing tuft of feathers on the head and lays up to 230 pretty pastel blue through to olive green eggs in a year.*

RESCUE BATTERY HENS

Intensively reared for the commercial market, these birds are passed on to local charities when past the peak of their productive lives, which is after about a year. They are generally free of charge and will inevitably arrive in poor condition. However, with a little care they can build up their health and reward your kindness with enough eggs for the average domestic household.

THREE BANTAMS

Smaller than regular hens, bantams will lay fewer eggs but are the perfect choice if you want a decorative selection of birds. Bantams are either miniature versions of larger hen breeds or true bantams with no counterpart. A distinguishing feature of many is the feathers on their legs, giving the appearance of flared trousers or a pair of ski boots.

PEKIN *A true bantam breed originating in Asia, this is a short-legged bird with long, soft feathers in a range of colours from black, white, blue, buff and cuckoo to the popular lavender colour. It will lay only about 60 beige eggs a year.*

SILVER-LACED SEBRIGHT *One of the most beautifully marked of all the breeds, this British-bred bantam also comes in a gold version. It lays a modest number of creamy-white eggs.*

SILKIE *A miniature version of the full-sized hen, the silkie has very fluffy plumage and a pom-pom of feathers on the head. With a tendency to broodiness, it can be used to hatch eggs for other breeds, although it will also lay around 100 eggs a year of its own. White is the most glamorous colour for this bird but it also comes in shades of black, blue, gold and partridge.*

GUINEA FOWL AND QUAIL

For something a bit different, why not try your hand at keeping some game birds? Guinea fowl, although rather flighty, have beautiful spotted plumes and will certainly alert you if a fox is around – hence they may suit country life rather than an urban environment, where close neighbours may object to their noise. They are excellent for the table. Quail are little game birds that are ideal for the smaller garden and best suited to keeping in a run to prevent them from flying away. At six weeks old they begin laying their pretty speckled eggs, perfect as canapés when boiled for no more than two minutes. They are also delicious table birds.

Henhouses

Most henhouses on the market today are timber structures, although colourful modern versions aimed at encouraging urban dwellers to participate in keeping a hen or two have recently appeared with great success. The Eglu is an innovative design by the Omlet company, which also produces the Beehaus beehive (see page 107). The coops are of lightweight polypropylene, making them easy to move around the garden and to clean, and are therefore less susceptible than wood to harbouring pests and diseases. The company supplies everything you will need to start, including the hens.

Alternatively, the hen-house is where you can let your imagination run wild. You could build your own or commission a bespoke coop from a carpenter, incorporating a few details inspired by the ornamental buildings of the *Ferme Ornée* (below) for example, as long as you ensure it complies with the needs of the hen, including a roosting bar, nesting boxes, good ventilation and insulation, and security from foxes. Various architectural styles could be employed to create an amusing folly out of the coop – perhaps a Gothic-style house with ogee windows and pop-hole, a Classical example with columns and a pediment, chinoiserie painted red and gold with a distinctive Chinese roof-line, or maybe a rustic henhouse in the manner of an 18th-century hermitage. Even references to shell-houses and grottoes could be achieved by using scallop shells, easily obtainable from fishmongers or restaurants, as roof tiles. More than any other feature of the self-sufficient garden, the henhouse lends itself to replicating the amusing follies of the past.

Whatever architectural style you plump for, your henhouse should be relatively mobile, especially if you are keeping only a few birds. This will lessen the risk of rats sensing the whereabouts of the chicken feed and will also ensure the run is on a fresh plot if the hens have to stay shut in for any length of time. It will also manure your garden evenly. Although the hens will have eaten the grass, it will grow back quickly once the run is moved on.

Inspiration can be taken from designs of the past. Here, architect John Plaw's Gothic-style poultry house, featured in his **Ferme Ornée** *(1795), were designed for 'a lady in the New Forest, and intended to be erected on a lawn, in front of a neat cottage villa'.*

The Dairy and ☙ Home Farm

Farm buildings on the
Godolphin Estate, Cornwall.

From April beginning, till Andrew be past,
So long with good huswife her dairy doth last;
Good milch-cow and pasture, good husbands provide,
The res'due, good husvives know best how to guide.

— THOMAS TUSSER, *Five Hundred Points of Good Husbandry* (1557)

Dairy and meat products have for centuries been the main source of protein in the British diet. In country estates these would have been produced in a specially equipped dairy or on the home farm. Dairy produce, together with eggs, was generally known as 'white meat'. Originally sheep or goats' milk was preferred to cows' milk, but this changed by the 17th century when every household would either own a cow if they could afford it or hire one for milking from a local farmer. Milk was converted into butter and cheese, which was a way of preserving milk by reducing its water content and compressing the curds into manageable shapes and sizes. Fresh milk was reserved for children, the very old and invalids, but rarely drunk in its raw state by adults in fashionable households, who preferred to drink it hot in possets, or to eat it in rich, creamy custards. With the spread of ice-houses in Georgian England, ice cream became the most fashionable of desserts at the dinner table.

The dairy itself, like the poultry yard, was a feminine affair, the domain of the mistress of the house. It flourished in the 18th century, when it was furnished with decorative wall tiles, marble work surfaces and fountains for cooling the temperature. This, together with the creamy delights produced in the dairy and the fresh-faced milkmaids who worked there, bestowed upon the place an air of intense romanticism in both real-life and fiction, as epitomised in Thomas Hardy's novel *Tess of the D'Urbervilles* (1891), in which the blossoming romance between Tess and her suitor Angel Clare is set within the bucolic confines of the dairy. Nevertheless, women took the management of rural affairs very seriously, as witnessed by Mr Downing, an American visitor to Wimpole Hall in Cambridgeshire in the mid-19th century:

I have been walking for several hours today through these beautiful grounds with the Countess of H, who though a most accomplished person in all other matters, has a knowledge of everything relating to rural life, that would be incomprehensible to most American ladies … every improvement or embellishment is planned under her special direction … there is no shrinking at barn-yards, no affected fear of cows, no ignorance of the dairy and poultry-yard.'

Dairy work even figured in ornamental ceramics designed for the most fashionable households, such as this example in Chirk Castle, Wrexham.

Although more often an independent building within the park, or attached to the house itself, the dairy was sometimes located within the home farm, as at Clumber Park in Nottinghamshire where the dairy was designed by the 9th Duchess of Norfolk as an ornamental component of Castle Farm.

The home farm superseded the deer park as the principle source of meat production and, along with the crops grown in the fields, produced food not only for the immediate household but for much of the local community. Taking an interest in designing and managing the farm became a gentlemanly pursuit and it was not long before pigs, cattle and sheep were bred to excessive sizes in order to win cups and rosettes at county shows. In the 19th century, landowners aspired to improve productivity on the farm by taking advantage of the technological and industrial revolution that was spreading throughout the country.

THE DAIRY

Until the 18th century, work in the dairy was seasonal as many cattle were slaughtered in the autumn (specifically on St Andrews Day, 30th November) due to lack of winter fodder. Although dairy work was considered a pleasant enough task, it had to follow a strict routine: cows were milked in the milking-parlour in the early morning, sometimes to the accompaniment of song which, it was said, enticed the cow to increase her yield. The milk would then be transported to the dairy for separating into curds and whey. A cool temperature and cleanliness were of paramount importance. Wooden utensils and earthenware pans were employed in the dairy in place of metal, which could taint the milk. Soap was never used for the same reason; instead salt was scrubbed into every surface with very hot water before being thoroughly rinsed away.

Dairies were usually built on the north-facing side of the house and fitted with easy-to-clean surfaces such as glazed tiles and marble. At Dyrham Park in Gloucestershire, the Dutch theme employed throughout the house is carried through to the dairy where

A close-up of the interior of the dairy at Dyrham Park, Gloucestershire. The fine Delft tiles seem to have been stripped off the walls of the old dairy, and relaid here when the dairy was moved in the 1840s.

KITCHEN GARDEN ESTATE

WEDGWOOD AND THE DAIRY

The pottery firm Wedgwood produced cream-coloured earthenware called 'queen's ware' which was ideal for use in the dairy. In 1767 Josiah Wedgwood wrote to his agent that 'Cream-colour Tyles are much wanted, and the consumption will be great for Dairies' and two years later he reported that 'Lady Gower will build a dairy on purpose to furnish it with Cream Colour if I will engage to make Tiles for the walls.' The company exploited the manufacture of tiles and creamware to great success, in most cases decorated with a naturalistic motif of trailing ivy leaves. The dairy at Althorp House in Northamptonshire, designed by Henry Holland in 1786 and decorated by Lavinia, wife of the 2nd Earl Spencer, still houses one of the most complete Wedgwood interiors, with ivy-patterned tiles and green and cream pots, also decorated with an ivy motif.

The dairy at Althorp House, Northamptonshire, designed in 1786, with Wedgwood pots and tiles.

the walls are lined with Delft tiles (left), which were the tile of choice until surpassed by the Wedgwoods creamware in the second half of the 18th century. The fountain in the middle of the room provided running water and helped to maintain a cool temperature of around 10°C (50°F). Stained glass was used in the windows to diffuse the sunlight, but conveniently became another opportunity for decoration. At Woburn Abbey in Bedfordshire, Henry Holland's Chinese-style dairy, built around 1788, had windows decorated with Chinese scenes of pagodas, mandarins, birds and insects.

A diversion for ladies

Overseeing the dairy was a fashionable pastime for a lady. In the 18th century, just as industrialisation was approaching, the highest-ranking ladies in the land saw in the dairy an opportunity to enhance the pastoral idyll of the new Arcadian landscape gardens. The dairy also provided a retreat for royalty weary of sophisticated court life. At the end of the 17th century Queen Mary, William III's consort, had an ornamental dairy at Hampton Court in Surrey, decorated with Delft ware. This royal approval gave the go-ahead for just about every duchess in the country to play the dairy maid. The Duchess of Lauderdale at nearby Ham House injected an element of humour in her dairy by using cast-iron cow's legs to support the marble worktops (below), while at Croome Park in Worcestershire the new model dairy, along with the menagerie and model farm, was a gift to Lady Coventry from her husband. The interior was designed by Robert Adam in 1763, although it was not completed until a decade later when accounts refer to a purchase of 'best white dutch tyles' to line the walls. Niches in the walls initially housed vases, later replaced with statues of the four seasons, and it was fitted out with an impressive collection of Wedgwood. Such attention to detail would have ensured that the dairy featured on a tour of the park, although sadly this dairy has not survived.

Such was the ornamental nature of the dairy that by 1832 the German traveller Prince Puckler-Muskau wrote to his wife:

The dairy is one of the principle decorations of an English park, and stands by itself quite away from the cow-house. It is generally an elegant pavilion, adorned with fountains, marble walls, and rare and beautiful porcelain; and its vessels, large and small filled with the most exquisite milk and its products in all their varieties.

The Duchess of Lauderdale's Dairy, at Ham House, Surrey. The work surface is supported by cast-iron legs complete with hooves, and tiles of typical Wedgwood style adorn the walls.

In an engraving from 1836 of Belvoir Castle in Leicestershire, the Duchess of Rutland's Gothic dairy provides a suitable backdrop for a picnic, being situated in a neatly tended area of the park next to the ornamental lake with the imposing castle in the distance.

At Uppark in West Sussex, in a reversal of fortunes, it was the turn of the dairy-maid to play the duchess, confirming the dairy as the most romantic place on the estate. Built in 1785 but redesigned by Humphrey Repton in 1812, the dairy was decorated with all the necessary fittings, stained-glass windows, a black-and-white marble floor and tiles decorated with ivy lining the walls. The landowner, old Sir Harry Fetherstonhaugh, still unmarried at the age of 70, passed the dairy on a perambulation around the park and was struck by the sweet singing of a girl within. Mary Ann Bullock, the 21-year-old owner of the fine voice, was initially the dairy maid's helper, but was soon promoted to running the dairy as Sir Harry's visits became more frequent. Eventually he was minded to ask for her hand in marriage, apparently rendering Mary Ann speechless. Sir Harry is said to have continued, 'Don't answer me now, but if you will have me, cut a slice out of the leg of mutton that is coming up for my dinner today.' This she duly did and was forthwith sent to Paris to be educated as a lady. In September 1825, true to his word, Sir Harry wed Mary Ann and lived happily with his young wife until he died at the age of 92, his wife remaining at Uppark until her death in 1875. The Uppark dairy survives to this day as one of the best examples in the possession of the National Trust.

As the 19th century drew to a close, milk became commercially available and the railways ensured the delivery of fresh milk throughout the country, rendering the household dairy obsolete.

A dairy that has changed little since it was built in 1780, designed by Henry Holland, can be seen at Berrington Hall in Herefordshire. It is said to be one of the finest examples of the Louis XIV style in Britain.

Produce from the dairy

There was, of course, no risk that toying in the dairy would cause the aristocratic chatelaines to suffer the calloused hands endured by the hard-working servant girls who toiled to make the vital produce for the kitchen. Butter and cheese were the staples of the medieval diet and never fell from favour. The Elizabethans loved creamy desserts, especially the curiously named 'cabbage cream' (layers of clotted cream interspersed with a sprinkling of sugar and flavoured with rosewater). By the 17th century butter was used extensively for sweet and savoury cooking, including cake- and pastry-making and frying, and was added to all forms of boiled food, either during cooking or before serving to improve the appearance and flavour. It was even melted into hot ale to make a popular night-time drink (see page 184).

Partial view of the dairy at Canons Ashby, Northamptonshire, showing the cheese press. Cheese has been a staple of the British diet since medieval times.

Influences from Continental Europe ensured that cheese continued to be used in cooking well into the Georgian era, appearing in sauces for cauliflower, cardoons and macaroni, and in informal meals such as omelettes and Welsh rabbit, or 'rarebit', which made its first appearance as a written recipe in *The Art of Cookery* by Hannah Glasse in 1747 and remains a constant supper-time dish today. At formal dinners a cheese course was served at the end of a meal with new varieties continually developed, such as Stilton, which the author Daniel Defoe described as the English Parmesan.

Cream continued to be widely consumed in Georgian Britain, enriching savoury fricassées, ragouts and all sorts of braised dishes, along with an endless list of desserts. Traditional favourites included frothy syllabubs, originally created by milking the cow straight into a bowl of wine (see page 76), snows (a dessert of egg whites and cream), and anything that wobbled, quivered or quaked such as flummeries (a sweet jelly made with cream) and blancmanges. Lady Wentworth's recipe book from Dunham Massey, written in the 1730s, includes instructions for 'A Shakeing Pudding' and five versions of 'Quaking Pudding' (below), all served with a little melted butter.

Wooden butter shapers were used to mould butter into appropriate shapes, while the cool marble surface helped to prevent the butter from melting during shaping.

Lady Wentworth's Quaking Pudding No. 2

Take one pint of cream and boil it with a little large mace, nutmeg and ginger, when it hath boiled a little take out the spice, and sweeten it with sugar to your taste, and let it stand till it be cold, take a quarter of a pound of blanched almonds, and beat 'em very small with a little rosewater, and a little cream, then take as much more grated bread as almonds, and five eggs, take out one of the whites, and beat them very well, and mix all together with a little ginger finely serced [sliced], and salt to your taste, you must flour your napkin well and not tye it too close up, this pudding must boil an hour and half, then take some butter, and beat it with a little water.

LADY WENTWORTH'S UNPUBLISHED RECIPE BOOK (C.1730), DUNHAM MASSEY, CHESHIRE

ICE HOUSES AND ICE CREAM

Ice houses had begun to appear in landowners' parks throughout Britain during the 17th century, in particular after the Restoration when exiled royalists returned to Britain from Europe, where they would have come across these ingenious refrigerators. Although the ice itself was not pure enough to be consumed directly, for example in drinks and desserts, ice houses revolutionised the way food could be stored and prepared. By filling a deep, subterranean, brick-lined circular pit with ice from ponds and lakes on the estate, a freezing chamber was created that would last for up to three years. Ice houses were about 6m (20ft) deep from the top of the dome and 3.6m (12ft) in diameter, and filling them in the perishing winter months was a dreaded task, not least because servants were liable to fall into the freezing water while gathering the ice. As it would last longer than any with impurities, only crystal-clear ice was used, broken into pieces and thrown into the pit lined with straw for insulation. At Killerton in Devon, it took 30 men five days to fill the ice house with 40 tonnes of ice.

The interior of the ice house at Ham House, Surrey, showing the domed brick-lined ceiling.

Ice houses were originally thatched to provide added insulation, but over the years the thatch has been lost and most ice houses are now identified by their dome-shaped roofs. At Croome Park in Worcestershire, the ice house has been re-thatched to convey the original appearance of the building.

With the advent of the ice house came a new exciting dessert: ice cream. A recipe for 'icy cream' first appeared in Britain in the 1660s; flavoured with orange-flower water, the cream would have been frozen in a lidded pan covered with a combination of ice, alum and saltpetre which was necessary to keep the mixture frozen. However, it was not until the mid-18th century that ice-cream recipes were perfected by stirring the mixture as it began to freeze, a technique developed in France at the end of the previous century. As French cuisine was embraced by Georgian high society, so the craze for ice cream made it the most fashionable dessert of the dinner table. Mary Smith, housekeeper for Admiral Lord Anson at Shugborough in Staffordshire and later for Sir William Blackett at Wallington Hall in Northumberland, published *The Complete Housekeeper* (1773), which contains several recipes for ice creams frozen in a variety of fruit moulds to make a breathtaking edible centrepiece at the table. Various fruit would flavour the ice cream in the summer; at other times of year burnt ice creams might be served. These were not burnt in the modern sense but made with a caramel.

Victorian ice-cream-making equipment in the dairy at Ham House, Surrey.

Additional ingredients such as almonds and filberts ensured a variety of flavours. One surprising recipe that would not look out of place at an avant-garde dinner party today is for Parmesan ice cream (below), from Frederick Nutt's *The Complete Confectioner* (1789).

Ice cream is as popular today as it was when first introduced. Although commercially produced in vast quantities it is very easy to make at home, especially with a basic ice-cream maker, which simply churns the mixture in a frozen chamber. The possibilities are endless for sweet and savoury courses: pepper, basil and even chilli ice cream are but a few mixtures with which to experiment.

Parmesan Cheese Ice Cream

Take six eggs, half a pint of syrup, and a pint of cream; put them into a stewpan and boil [simmer] them until it begins to thicken; then rasp three ounces of parmesan cheese, mix and pass them through a sieve, and freeze it.

FREDERICK NUTT, *The Complete Confectioner* (1789)

The home farm

By the Georgian period, the home farm was held in as high regard by the country gentleman as the dairy was by his wife. Although animals had always been kept by cottagers and gentry alike to provide meat for the table, it was not until the agricultural advancements of the 18th and 19th centuries that farming was elevated to a suitable pastime for a gentleman. In 1833 John Loudon advocated that 'Every country gentleman … be a farmer to a certain extent; the size of his farm to be determined by the wants of his family.' From the Middle Ages, barns and other ancillary buildings were arranged around or next to the manor house, while the deer park was the living larder,

Highland cattle in a barn at Wimpole Home Farm, Cambridgeshire, which was designed by prestigious architect Sir John Soane in 1794.

supplying all the meat for the household. However, during the 18th century, with the emerging division between the aesthetic and productive estate, the home farm evolved into a separate entity. Although utilitarian in concept, it was very much a status symbol where the latest farming methods and exotic breeds such as the highly prized white cattle were shown off to visiting guests. This is reflected in the choice of fashionable architects who were commissioned to design the buildings. At Wimpole in Cambridgeshire, for example, the home farm was rebuilt in 1794 to the designs of Sir John Soane, and in 1805 at Shugborough, Staffordshire, Samuel Wyatt was the architect.

Prime cuts

A result of this interest in farming was the significant improvement in the quality of meat. Previously, meat was preserved by salting or smoking to ensure a supply during the winter. In the 17th century cattle and sheep were marched in droves to the London markets to feed the growing urban population. The exhausted beasts inevitably arrived in a poor state to be slaughtered in often squalid conditions, providing a tough and often diseased meat to the consumer, all of which did nothing for the reputation of British food. However, by the following century, the gentlemanly concern for farming gave rise to a competitive interest in breeding the perfect beast, fat and flavoursome. Animals were taken to local shows and wagers made on who would win the coveted prize. Exaggerated images of pigs and cattle were captured on canvas as an enduring reminder of the magnificent beasts, one of the most famous being the Airedale Heifer from East Riddlesden Hall, West Yorkshire (below). This prize-winning animal weighed a record 299kg (660lb) per quarter when it was slaughtered, with 28cm (11in) of fat measured at the ribs.

The improvements paid off as Britain became renowned for the quality of its meat, satirised by William Hogarth in his painting *The Gate of Calais* or *O, the Roast Beef of Old England* (1748). In the scene, a huge side of beef is being carried from the harbour to an English tavern, watched by a hungry group of French soldiers and a rotund friar, drooling as he watches it pass. Such was the reputation of the British roast that the French even nicknamed the British citizens *les rosbifs*.

Images of prize-winning animals, such as **The Airedale Heifer** *(1830), were testament to their success.*

Roast Ribs of Beef

INGREDIENTS
Beef, a little salt.

TIME
10 lb. of beef, 2½ hours; 14 to 16 lbs., from 3½ to 4 hours

AVERAGE COST
8½ d. per lb.

SUFFICIENT
A joint of 10 lb. sufficient for 8 or 9 persons.

SEASONABLE
At any time

MODE – The fore-rib is considered the primest roasting piece, but the middle-rib is considered the most economical. Let the meat be well hung (should the weather permit), and cut off the thin ends of the bones, which should be salted for a few days, and then boiled. Put the meat down to a nice clear fire, put some clean dripping into the pan, dredge the joint with a little flour, and keep continually basting the whole time. Sprinkle some fine salt over it (this must never be done until the joint is dished, as it draws the juices from the meat); pour the dripping from the pan, put in a little boiling water slightly salted, and strain the gravy over the meat. Garnish with tufts of scraped horseradish, and send horseradish sauce to table with it. A Yorkshire pudding sometimes accompanies this dish, and, if lightly made and well cooked, will be found a very agreeable addition.

ISABELLA BEETON, *The Book of Household Management* (1861)

A view of some 1465ha. (3620 acres) of farm and woodlands of Coleshill, Wiltshire. The farmhouse is of Cotswold stone and tile, and typical of the region.

The model farm

The model farm came to signify the 18th-century ideals of the Enlightenment – to be beautiful as well as utilitarian, while improving the welfare standards of the farm workers. At a time of agricultural prosperity and innovation it was designed to make use of the latest agricultural practices and technologies, both in building design and livestock husbandry.

One of the most revolutionary examples was at Coleshill in Wiltshire (above), where a model farm was established in 1854. Its layout was innovative yet practical and the design was notable for the use of sloping and split-level sites. The farm buildings were designed for a mixed farming system, including grain, root crops and various livestock enterprises. Cattle, sheep and pigs, in which the Earl of Radnor took special interest, were bred, fattened and over-wintered in the buildings. Stock feed and manure was distributed around the farm along tramways that made use of the gradients. The farm was mainly horse-powered, although steam-power was used in the granary and mixing room. Today, the model farm remains well preserved and open to the public, with produce for sale in the local estate shop.

The *ferme ornée*

The *ferme ornée* was a French term adopted to describe the 18th-century fashion for ornamental farms situated within the parks of country houses. Despite the French name, the style was essentially British. Ornamental planting of hedgerows and flowerbeds were as much part of the concept as picturesque barns and bothys. Early farms that exemplified the idea were Woburn Farm in Surrey, which Philip Southcote purchased in 1734, and the poet William Shenstone's The Leasowes in Shropshire, which covered an area of 61ha (150 acres), of which 14ha (35 acres) were given over as pleasure grounds, the rest divided into two-thirds pasture and one-third arable, although the ornamental theme of flowering shrubs and trees was carried through the whole, united by a continuous path.

George III had a celebrated *ferme ornée* at Kew near London and, as the fashion for the informal English style of gardening took hold in France, Marie Antoinette created the most famous example of all at Versailles in the form of le Petit Hameau, built in 1783–87. With little intent for food production, it was a pastoral retreat for the Queen who, stifled by formal court life, could fancy herself a milkmaid or shepherdess. The architect John Plaw's pattern book, *Ferme Ornée* (1795), contains an eclectic mix of designs for domestic agricultural and estate buildings, from cattle sheds to cottages and dairy houses to dog-kennels, in Gothic, Classical or Rustic styles.

The blossoming tree, wild flowers and rustic fence of the landscape in this idealised illustration of a shepherd and shepherdess by Kate Greenaway (1876) conveys the qualities of the ferme ornée from a hundred years earlier.

Profitable pigs

Pigs were one of the most useful animals, providing pork for eating fresh and for preserving as ham and bacon. They were kept by gentry and peasants alike and were cheap to maintain as they fed on household waste. In his *Country Housewife's Family Companion* (1750) William Ellis described bacon as 'serviceable, palatable, profitable, and clean Meat, for a ready Use in a Country House' and 'universally traded in ... and ... serviceable to both rich and poor'.

Cottagers commonly kept a pig in the back yard for slaughtering in the autumn. When cured for bacon it would last long enough to feed the family throughout the winter months. The traditional country labourers' breakfast consisted of bacon and fried potatoes left over from the night before, while the children's share would be the tasty dripping soaked in bread. Even in the first half of the 20th century, keeping a pig was not uncommon for country folk such as Betty Tremlin, who grew up in rural Gloucestershire where her parents ran the local pub. She recalls her childhood in the early part of the 20th century when the family kept a couple of cows for milk and a pig for bacon, as well as numerous chickens. The pig was butchered at home and the two sides laid out on a slate slab and salted regularly until they were cured. The meat was then wrapped before it was stored and the following account illustrates how nothing was wasted in the procedure:

The muslin came from the butcher who used to get their imported lambs covered in it and would let Mother have some. She would boil them to get all the blood out, and then when they were perfectly white she would wrap them around the bacon sides and that would protect the meat from flies. The finer muslin she would keep and use to strain the milk through. The milk was never cooled, it was brought in the buckets from the cows and ... poured into the big pans through the muslin. It was fresh every day, and any left-over milk was fed to the pigs. I was brought up on everything they tell you today that you shouldn't eat ... thick cream, puddings with custard and fruit from the orchard with thick creamy rice pudding.

While many great estates gave up their farms as commercial food production increased, several country folk still kept a pig and a cow for milking well into the 20th century, curing their own bacon and ham. However, bureaucratic intervention today has made it very complicated to keep livestock in domestic situations. County Parish Holding Numbers are required and arrangements need to be made for slaughtering and butchering, as legislation prohibits the slaughter of animals at home.

TODAY'S ALTERNATIVES

For most people keeping pigs is not a practical option, since good husbandry requires more time, effort and knowledge than many can afford. For those who are not deterred, one animal that seems to adapt well to being kept in a domestic situation, albeit a well-fenced one, is a goat, which can supply you with nourishing low-cholesterol meat containing around half the calories of lamb, or, if kept for dairy, one of the most wholesome milks available.

Even with cow's milk from the milkman, children can spend many determined hours shaking the creamy top of the milk in a jar, waiting for the moment when a ball of butter appears. Cheese-making at home, however, is a messy business unless you have the luxury of a cool and airy room to put aside for dairy work, fitted out to the same principles as in the past with easy-to-clean surfaces and a water source, and will probably be undertaken only by the most ambitious self-sufficient enthusiasts.

Pigmy goats and pigs are a popular choice as pets and will bestow a flavour of the *ferme ornée* to any garden, especially if housed in an appropriately ornate ark or barn, while keeping you in touch with the origins of the food on your plate.

Traditional breeds such as Gloucester Old Spot pigs are once again being reared for their flavoursome meat.

The Deer Park and Game

'A park replete with deer and conies is a necessary and pleasant thing.'

— ANDREW BOORDE, *A Dyetary of Helth* (1542)

Fallow deer in the park at Knole, Kent.

Deer parks have always been regarded as the ultimate status symbol for the aristocracy because of their association with the princely sport of hunting. In medieval images they were depicted as an earthly paradise, while deer were bestowed with moral and religious symbolism, stags in particular representing immortality. Until the 17th century deer parks were the preserve of the monarch, and anyone wishing to empark their land was obliged to obtain a licence; failure to do so could result in a hefty fine.

Soon every ambitious landowner aspired to owning a deer park. In 1617 the Elizabethan traveller Fynes Moryson noted in *Itinerary*:

The English are so naturally inclined to pleasure, as there is no Countrie, wherein the Gentlemen and Lords have so many and large Parkes onely reserved for the pleasure of hunting, or where all sorts of men alot so much ground about their houses for pleasure of Gardens and Orchards.'

Not only deer, but grazing cattle and sheep, rabbit warrens, fish ponds and dovecotes were commonly situated within the park, as well as horses, the essential means of transport. All were securely enclosed by the park pale – a ditch and bank construction topped with a cleft oak fence. An occasional deer-leap may have interrupted the pale, allowing deer to inadvertently enter the park but not to escape.

Although not an indigenous species, by the 18th century the pheasant had become one of the most prolific game birds in Britain, and remains so today.

THE LIVING LARDER

A few parks, such as those belonging to royalty or wealthy aristocrats, were exceptionally large, some comprising a thousand hectares or more. The majority, however, were of a more modest 40ha (100 acres) in size, some no larger than 20ha (50 acres). Deer were the most prestigious animal to be kept, particularly fallow deer, said to have been introduced by the Romans and with a temperament better suited to domestication than the native red or roe deer. White deer were especially revered, while exotic species of deer might be kept as a curiosity. Kip's bird's-eye view of Rycote House in Oxfordshire from *Britannia Illustrata* (1707), for example, features an 'East India Deer Park' recalling the exotic menageries of the early medieval pleasances, or pleasure parks. The fashion for exotic deer peaked

in the early 1900s, when the Duke of Bedford kept about 40 species in his park at Woburn. At least ten different species can still be seen there today.

Deer meat derived the name of venison from the Latin *venari*, meaning 'to hunt'. During the Middle Ages it would have been available only to royalty and the nobility and would have been reserved for occasions such as royal visits, or presented as a gift. Venison was rarely bought or sold on the open market and for anyone caught poaching the penalties were severe. Legend has it that the young William Shakespeare was apprehended while poaching deer in Sir Thomas Lucy's park at Charlecote in Warwickshire. Some say he was flogged, causing him to flee to London where he began his writing career in earnest. He exacted his revenge on Sir Thomas, thinly veiled as Justice Shallow, in *The Merry Wives of Windsor*.

As the rules began to relax, it became possible to hunt deer legally from a neighbouring park if payments were made to the park keeper. Venison gradually became more widely available and was served with increased regularity at the dinner table. It even began to appear on the menu at taverns around the country. Samuel Pepys makes frequent references in his diaries to enjoyable meals of venison, usually when dining with friends but occasionally at local hostelries: at the Cock Pit he ate 'rare pot venison, and ale to abundance till almost twelve at night', and on another occasion, at the Bullhead, he was full of praise when he dined upon 'the best venison pasty that ever I eat of in my life'. The best cuts were roasted, others were boiled or stewed, occasionally with the addition of wine to tenderise the meat.

~ RECIPE ~

Roast Venison

After you have washed your venison clear from the blood, stick it with cloves on the outside and lard it with mutton lard or porke lard, but mutton is the best. Then spit it and rost it by a socking [slow] fire. Take vinegar, bread crums and the gravy which comes from the venison and boil them in a dishe, then season it with sugar, cinnamon, ginger and salt, and serve the venison upon the sauce.

RECIPE FROM A MANUSCRIPT AT ERDDIG, WREXHAM (1686)

DECLINE AND DESTRUCTION

The economic pressures of the early 17th century resulted
in a decline in some of the smaller deer parks, considered
unprofitable for their owners since they were prohibited by law
from selling the venison. This forced some to turn their parks
over to the more profitable cattle or sheep, as Richard Carew noted
in his survey of Cornwall in 1602: 'Deere leap over the pale to give
the bullockes place.' The parks that did survive belonged to the
wealthiest landowners, thus reinforcing the park as a status symbol,
and as such they were a natural target for the Parliamentarians
during the Civil War. The Parliamentarian soldier Nehemiah
Wharton recorded the destruction of several deer parks in his
letters, including Sir Francis Leigh's parks at Newnham Regis
in Warwickshire. His satisfaction at consuming the forbidden
meat is evident. On 30th August 1642 he wrote:

*Fryday several of our soldiers, both horse and foote sallied out of the city unto the Lord
Dunmore's park, and brought from thence great store of venison, which is as good as ever
I tasted, and ever since they make it their dayly practise, so that venison is almost as
common with us as beefe with you.*

Death of a Buck
*(c.1660) by an unknown
artist at Lyme Park, Cheshire.*

The plunder and general
destruction of the parks was
a symbolic gesture against the
crown and nobility and many
royal parks were sold off for
public use, including Charles
I's new park at Richmond,
which was given to the City
of London.

Not surprisingly, the
creation of parks did not
feature greatly during the
Commonwealth period.
However, with the Restoration
of the monarchy in 1660, there
came a renewed interest in
hunting as a celebrated pastime
of the landed classes. Although

THE DEER PARK AND GAME

many parks were restored, they took on a more ornamental role than previously. The park gradually came to be seen as an extension of the garden with the introduction of allées, bosquets, wildernesses and, most enduringly, the avenue, which has remained a symbolic statement of arrival in landscape design to this day.

By the early 18th century, the era of the grand formal garden came to a close. Bird's-eye views of many estates throughout the country were drawn up by the engraver and draughtsman team of Kip and Knyff (above), depicting manor houses set within their formal estates surrounded by deer parks. These images provide a valuable source of evidence that shows how the estates were arranged before the English landscape movement swept away all the geometry a few years later.

Bishop Pococke's 1750s account of Lyme Park in Cheshire describes a neglected park that was once evidently a great ornamental landscape with large expanses of water and avenues typical of the late 17th century:

I went to the park and house of mr Leigh of Lyme; the situation is extraordinary, the park being on a declivity up the side of those hills, on which are the bounds between Cheshire and Derbyshire, it extends also to the west on the other side of the valley of the foot of the hills … There is one picture in the house of Watson, a park keeper, who is 104 years old and now alive, having been in that office ever since 1674, and has seen five generations hunt in the park; behind the house is a large piece of black water, with wood behind it, and to the west a hanging garden, now neglected, which goes down to the vale; but the great curiosity of this place are the red deer, the stags are brought together before the house and being drove gently up to the pond they swim through it, and it is an extraordinary sight to see their horns like a wood moving along the water ... There are no buildings in the park, except one, which at a distance has the appearance of an obelisk and an old castle whited up, which is seen at a great distance. All the avenues to the park are lock'd, and no one is admitted but with somebody that is known, unless they have the weekly watchword.

The 'old castle' building probably referred to the 'cage', a hunting tower built in 1737 that replaced an earlier building (below left). The sight of the deer being driven through the water refers to the annual summer counting of the red stags by driving them across the pond, a scene captured in a lithograph from c.1750 (see below).

Lithograph of the Deer Park at Lyme, Cheshire (c.1750), showing the midsummer custom of driving stags through the Stag Pool to count them.

THE LANDSCAPE PARK

The 18th century witnessed a dramatic decline in the number of deer parks for a variety of reasons, including land enclosures and the industrialisation of many parts of Britain. The fox became the principle quarry for the hunt in most parts of the country, consigning deer parks to a new role as an idealised, Arcadian setting for the new Classical mansions that were being built. The reinvented deer park bestowed on the estate an air of venerability and antiquity

A stag roaring during rutting at Lyme Park, Cheshire.

and the deer were retained for ornamental purposes. The overall scene was enhanced by the innovation of the ha-ha, a concealed ditch and wall that formed an invisible boundary between the pleasure grounds and park when viewed from the house.

A few parks had ornamental deer-cotes designed for winter feeding. A particularly fine towering example was designed by Samuel Wyatt in 1767 for Lord Scarsdale at Kedleston Hall in Derbyshire, although sadly it was never built. The large, imposing, though less fanciful, deer barn at Dunham Massey in Cheshire, built in 1740, has, however, survived intact. Despite their ornamental role, deer were still a valuable source of meat, although by now they were usually culled by the park keeper for use in the kitchen, rather than hunted as before.

Today, most of the smaller parks of the gentry estates are no longer to be seen but ancient trees and browsing lines, together with keepers' lodges and viewing towers, remain iconic and enduring features of Britain's unique parkland heritage.

KITCHEN GARDEN ESTATE

Rabbit warrens

Many deer parks contained a warren, originally meaning an area in which the landowner could hunt small game such as rabbits, hares and pheasants. Rabbits had been introduced to Britain from the Mediterranean by the Normans in the 12th century, and were highly prized for both their meat and their fur; unlike deer, which were rarely bought or sold, they were also a source of income. Because they originated from warmer climates it was thought they needed protection from the harsh British weather and therefore were kept in specially constructed warrens consisting of earthworks known as 'pillow mounds', each housing as many as 80 rabbits. These flat-topped banks were sometimes arranged in complex patterns of squares or crosses, remains of which can still be seen in parks and forests throughout Britain today, with particularly well-defined examples surviving at Hatfield Forest in Essex. Ferrets would have been used to flush out the rabbits which, in their attempt to escape, were trapped in nets stretched over the burrows.

Like deer, rabbits had their own keeper, or warrener, to protect them from poachers. The warrener's lodge, located within the warren, would have doubled up as an architectural feature in the park. The most elaborate surviving example is Thomas Tresham's Triangular Lodge at Rushton in Northamptonshire, completed in 1595. Set in a warren of over 121ha (300 acres) and designed and decorated as a monument to Catholicism, it nevertheless conveys the high status of rabbits during this period, as reinforced by various writers including Andrew Boorde, who stated that 'rabbits flesh is best of all wild beasts'. Rabbit meat was generally used in pottages or stews, or, if eaten whole, it might be 'given a pudding in his belly', that is, stuffed with bread, suet, herbs and spices before being roasted in the same way as whole fish (see page 118). Rabbit was a favourite of Henry VII, who enforced a 'close' season of several months when they could not be hunted to ensure their survival. Such was their popularity that Thomas Moffett, writing in the late

Photograph of Mr Kidwell the Gamekeeper at Arlington Court, Devon.

Rabbits were highly prized for both their meat and their fur throughout the 16th and 17th centuries but by the end of the 18th century they had become so commonplace that their meat was deemed fit only for peasants.

16th century, felt rabbits were consumed more widely by the English than any other nation.

The numbers of rabbit warrens increased in the 17th century and in many cases would have been rented out to neighbouring farmers. At Felbrigg Hall in Norfolk, the warren was let to one Thomas Gosse, who agreed to supply William Wyndham with 300 rabbits a year and to leave the warren with 1300 'breeding conies' when his lease expired. Selling rabbits was a lucrative business; in 1628 at Knole in Kent, the revenue from rabbit sales contributed to one-fifth of the estate's total income for that year.

By the 18th century the number of rabbits had increased to such an extent that coursing – catching rabbits with dogs – was a popular pastime. In 1778 Parson Woodforde noted in his diary:

Soon after breakfast I walked out a Coursing and took Ben and Boy [his greyhounds] with me, we did not return til near three … we had tolerable Sport, coursed one Hare and a Couple of Rabbitts, all of whom we killed, it was a very large hare.

In 1792 Viscount Torrington visited Lyme Park in Cheshire, four decades after Bishop Pococke wrote his account, and commented on its further decline: 'Most of the Park is a dreary waste, abandoned to rabbits.' By now the rapidly increasing number of rabbits meant that their meat had lost its status and had become commonplace, fit only for peasants. Despite this, about 30 recipes featured in the late 19th-century editions of Isabella Beeton's *The Book of Household Management*, proving that rabbit meat remained a popular staple of the middle-class diet. The 20th century, however, witnessed a rapid decline in the popularity of rabbit, a direct result of myxomatosis, a disease misguidedly introduced to control their numbers.

DUCK DECOYS

The Decoy (c.1670), one
of a series of hunting scenes
painted by Francis Barlow.

The park provided an ideal habitat for the rearing of game birds.
Early methods of catching birds included trapping with nets or
hunting with hawks until the 19th century. Ducks were frequently
trapped in a specially designed decoy, a device introduced from
Holland, the name having its origins in the Dutch *de kooi*, meaning
'the cage'. Wild fowl would be lured on to the pond by a 'fake' duck,
then herded into a wickerwork tunnel by the decoyman and his dog
and trapped inside, to be taken for the kitchen when required. From
the cook's point of view trapping ducks this way was preferable to
shooting them, as it ensured the flesh would be free from shot.

Kip's bird's-eye view of Guisborough Priory in Yorkshire from
1707 depicts a pyramidal duck decoy on a pond, and a similar one
is depicted in a painting from c.1670 by Francis Barlow for Denzil
Onslow at Clandon Park in Surrey (above). A surviving 17th-century
duck decoy can be seen at Boarstall in Buckinghamshire.

GAME AND THE SPORTING GUN

Improvements in the sporting gun towards the end of the 17th century resulted in a dramatic rise in the popularity of the shoot as a sporting pastime. Large numbers of birds were raised within the parks specifically for the purpose, and wooded areas planted to provide ideal game cover, with evergreen trees in particular. The archetypal features of the 18th-century landscape park, such as hill-top coverts, belts and scattered clumps of woodland, were designed not only as an aesthetic improvement but to benefit this increasingly fashionable sport.

In the 18th century, although the most coveted game birds were partridge, grouse, plover, quail, lapwing, woodcock, snipe and teal, the pheasant was the bird most suited to the sport and bred in such quantities that in 1787, on a visit to Blenheim Palace in Oxfordshire, Viscount Torrington commented: 'In various parts of the park … [are] clusters of faggots around a coop, where are hatched and reared such quantities of pheasants that I almost trod upon them in the grass.' Fewer smaller birds than in previous centuries were taken, although larks were an exception to the rule, according to an inventory of 1760 from the Shugborough estate in Staffordshire which lists 15 lark-spits.

The scullery at Llanerchaeron, Ceredigion, was used for preparing food such as ducks, pheasants, rabbits and other game.

RECIPE

Woodcock Soup

Take half a dozen woodcocks and after you've feathered them cut off the heads and feet. Then take and bruise 'em in a marble mortar till they are pretty small and grate in a penny loaf. Then have in readiness some good broth either made with beef or mutton, and put them into it and let it boil a good while. Then take it off and strain it through a cullender and put in a pint of claret and give it a heat. Then take a roast woodcock and put in the middle of your dish with the heads and all the rest stuck in it, and take the feet to garnish the dish with sippets between.

LADY WENTWORTH'S UNPUBLISHED RECIPE BOOK (C.1730),
DUNHAM MASSEY, CHESHIRE

Game needs to be hung for between two days and three weeks to enable the meat proteins to break down, thus removing the gamey taste that many find objectionable and tenderising the meat. To accommodate this, some estates had special game larders situated away from the house to avoid the unpleasant smell of hanging game. A pulley would haul the game up to hang between ventilators in the roof, gauzed to protect the meat from flies. There are good examples at Kedleston Hall in Derbyshire and at Uppark in West Sussex. At Farnborough Hall in Oxfordshire the game larder (right) was designed by the 18th-century gentleman architect Sanderson Miller, with Tuscan columns, considered the appropriate order for rural buildings, and a loggia overlooking the 17th-century fish ponds.

The Edwardian period was a time when large, expensive shoots flourished on many estates with the royal seal of approval from the King, a keen shot himself. During the shooting season between August and February the sport was taken to excess, with thousands of birds shot in a single day for consumption at the countless dinner parties held for the occasion.

The hexagonal game larder at the end of the terrace at Farnborough Hall, Oxfordshire. Its four sturdy columns provide a loggia overlooking a series of walled paddocks and some original 17th-century fish ponds.

A FREE-RANGE OPTION

Today, as in the past, a deer park is beyond the means of all but a few people. However, in contrast to its past exclusive status, venison is now available to all, as an economic alternative to beef and lamb. Deer are now rarely hunted with hounds; instead, since the early 1970s, they have been farmed for their meat, initially in Scotland and now all over Britain, often in the existing parkland originally designed for the purpose. While the elitist connotation of a deer park is set deep within our consciousness, existing deer parks can offer truly local seasonal meat that was once the preserve of only the wealthiest citizens and is now available to all. Today there are over 360 deer farms in Great Britain farming around 30,000 deer. This produces an average of 500 tonnes of venison annually.

The shoot remains part of the economy of private estates during the autumn and winter months, as corporations and individuals are willing to pay well for a day's sport. At this time of year the fallen game birds are plentiful and inexpensive and provide a richer-flavoured alternative to the ubiquitous chicken. Rabbit, however, has never regained its former popularity and status.

Hop Gardens
and Vineyards

'There are a hundred … sorts of beer made in England; and some not bad:
Art has well supply'd Nature in this particular.'

— FRANCOIS MISSON, *Memoires et Observatins faites par un Voyageur en Angleterre* (1698)

Clusters of hop flowers
on the inner wall of the
walled garden at Oxburgh
Hall, Norfolk.

In Britain today everyone has access to safe, clean drinking water, but that has not always been the case. In an age before purification, untreated water was hazardous to drink, causing fatal diseases such as cholera and typhoid. Fermented drinks such as beer, wine and cider were safer alternatives. Wine was the preserve of the wealthy, while beer was commonly consumed by all classes of society. 'Small beer', a sweetened low-alcohol variety, was even given to children as it was considered nutritious. Beer was the most usual drink in many country households until the First World War, being cheaper than tea which was, until relatively recently, a luxury commodity.

BEER

Brewing is an ancient skill, even preceding the Roman occupation. Despising the native drink, the Romans set about establishing vineyards to make wine, a familiar drink from their homeland. Although they did cultivate hops, this was not for brewing but as a vegetable crop and they remained a popular dish well into the early 19th century, when the rural commentator William Cobbett described hop shoots as 'a delightful a vegetable as ever was put on a table, not yielding, during about the three weeks that it is in season, to the asparagus itself'. A traditional Kentish way of serving them was to harvest young shoots in spring when just a few centimetres high, boil them in broth and eat like asparagus with buttered toast. The versatility of hops is apparent from a variety of other practical applications: they were made into a yellow dye for wool, the oil was used in perfumery and the stems could be made into coarse cloth used for sacking, as instructed by the 17th-century landowner Sir John Oglander in his *Commonplace Book*.

Cut your hop-stalks off a yard in length as soon as you gather your hops. Then open the stalks and bind them in bundles at either end and lay them in water for nine days. Then take them out and dry them on a kiln till the wood grows very brittle, so that the bark will peel easily from it. Then strip it and use it as you do hemp.

It was not until the end of the 15th century, however, that hops were used in brewing to make beer, influenced by Flemish refugees who settled in Britain, bringing with

Brewing was once an honourable occupation, depicted here in a detail of 16th or 17th century painted glass at Oxburgh Hall, Norfolk.

Oasthouse at Bateman's, East Sussex. A common sight in south-east England, oasthouses are a testament to the importance of brewing.

them their brewing techniques. Hops were added to improve the flavour of ale, originally a strong, sweet brew made with malted barley and flavoured with spices, herbs and even tree bark. Since hops contain antiseptic resins, they also acted as a preservative, increasing the shelf life of the brew, which had the effect of upping the alcohol content. Despite early attempts to maintain a distinction between ale and beer, the latter gradually superseded the traditional ale, and the two names have now become interchangeable. In Tudor times, hot buttered beer made with the addition of spices, eggs and butter was a popular winter beverage (below). Although almost forgotten in Britain today, the legacy of buttered drinks continues in the USA, where hot buttered rum is traditionally consumed at Christmas time.

Hops would have been cultivated in hop gardens, the flowers gathered in the early autumn and then dried in either bread ovens or oast houses. They were used straight away for a strong brew or stored for up to a year to make a lighter drink.

In *The English Husbandman* (1613), Gervase Markham regarded hops as 'of greate use an commoditie in this kingdom' and advised planting the hop-garden:

Neare as you can place it near some cover, or shelter, as either of hils, houses, high-walls, woods or trees ... also the nearer it is planted to your dwelling house it is so much the better, both because the vigilance of your own eye is a good guarde thereunto, and also the labours of your work-master will be the more careful and diligent.

Such vigilance indicates that hops were a highly valued crop with commercial production centred on certain regions such as Herefordshire and Kent.

Buttered Beer

Take beer or ale and boil it, then scum it, and put to it some liquorish and anniseeds, boil them well together; then have in a clean flaggon or quart pot some yolks of eggs well beaten with some of the foresaid beer, and some good butter; strain your butter'd beer, put it in the flaggon, and brew it with the butter and eggs.

ROBERT MAY, *The Accomplisht Cook* (1664)

The business of brewing

Despite the fact that beer was available from inns and taverns throughout the country, it made economic sense for large households to brew their own. Many country houses were therefore furnished with a brew-house and hop garden. Sir John Oglander advised his household, 'Brew thy beer and be sure to hop and boil it well, and of two bushels of malt and one of oats make 14 barrels of beer.' Brew-houses were usually situated next to the bake-house, as the two shared common facilities and ingredients such as ovens and yeast. The waste malt would be fed to the pigs, with the occasional inadvertent consequence, as Parson Woodford recorded in his diary in 1778:

The brew house at Charlecote Park, Warwickshire. A typical brew-house of a well-ordered English country seat during the late 18th century, used to brew beer for the household until the early 20th century.

My two large Piggs, by drinking some beer grounds ... got so amazingly drunk ... that they were not able to stand and appeared like dead things almost. I never saw Piggs so drunk in my life — I slit their ears for them without feeling.

The following morning the pigs were 'still unable to walk yet ... they tumble about the yard & can by no means stand at all steady yet'. It took them until the afternoon to sober up.

Traditionally, as indoor work, brewing was considered a woman's task, although in large establishments it was customary for a man to be employed as brewer, an esteemed role rewarded with a higher wage even than the cook. By the 1800s beer was regarded principally as a drink for the servants, valued for its nutritional qualities, and essential to the diet of hard-working labourers, to whom it was served at every meal, including breakfast. It was frequently given in lieu of wages; at Shugborough in Staffordshire, accounts from 1819 indicate that the household consumed around 109 litres (24 gallons) of beer a day, with the head laundry maid receiving 2.3 litres (½ gallon) a day! In 1822, at Dunham Massey in Cheshire, the 20 or so resident servants consumed one 273 litres (60 gallons) barrel of beer every week, averaging 2 litres (3½ pints) a day, although in reality men were allocated twice the amount as women.

By the 18th century, the growth of commercial breweries in urban regions heralded the decline in home-brewed ales, although the tradition continued in rural areas well into the 1800s. The eccentric

The brewery at Lacock Abbey, Wiltshire. The brewery is probably 16th century with later additions and was in use until the 18th century.

Sir Henry Dryden of Canons Ashby in Northamptonshire, a keen maker of home-brewed beer, would dress up as a tramp and invite travellers back to his ancient kitchen to taste his particular blend, spiked with bicarbonate of soda for 'extra fizz'!

Country-dwellers continued the tradition of home-brewing until the early 20th century, since beer remained beneficial to the household economy. It not only served as a nutritious drink but could be used to cure ham and, where beeswax was not available, served as an effective stain and polish for country furniture. On top of that, women found that washing their hair with beer made it shine.

There were usually two brewings a year, one before harvest and another for Christmas. Farm labourers were given an allowance of hops and malt, while the yeast would be borrowed from a neighbour in a prearranged agreement as part of a 'yeast-chain'. The process took a day and a night to complete and demanded keen vigilance, as it would be a great loss to the household if the beer spoiled. Although home brewing continues today as a hobby, it is generally carried out with the use of kits containing pre-packaged ingredients.

KITCHEN GARDEN ESTATE

VINEYARDS

Vines have a more romantic appeal than hops, having associations with both classical antiquity and biblical stories. Introduced to Britain by the Romans, they have had a chequered history, as their success is dependent on climatic conditions, among other factors. Before the Norman Conquest, vines were cultivated in monastic establishments in southern England for the communion ceremony. It is a matter of conjecture how much wine was produced from the vineyards. White grape varieties were better suited to the British climate, so it is likely that most red wine would have needed to be imported; the marriage of Henry II and Eleanor of Aquitaine in 1152 initiated large-scale imports of wine from France.

Wine was generally the preserve of wealthy households and was originally served from the wooden cask, glass bottles appearing on the scene around 1658. A sweetened spiced wine called hippocras, or *ipocras*, was enjoyed as an after-dinner digestive from the medieval period up until the 18th century (below). The choice of spices would have included cinnamon, cloves, ginger, nutmeg, pepper, and grains of paradise, similar to pepper and, although little known today, an Elizabethan favourite. The spice-infused wine would then be filtered through a jelly bag, known to apothecaries as a *manicum hippocraticum* – the sleeve of Hippocrates, giving the drink its name.

Detail of one of the 'Months' tapestries (1699–1719) by Stephen de May, at Ham House, Surrey. This detail is from The Vintage for the month of October.

To Make *Ipocras*

Take a gallon of claret or white wine and put therein 4 ounces of ginger, and ounce and half of nutmegs, of cloves, an quarter of Sugar, 4 pound. Let all this stand together in a pot at least twelve houers, then take it and put it in a clere bage made for the purpose so that the wine may come with good coller from the wine.

RECIPE FROM A MANUSCRIPT AT ERDDIG, WREXHAM (1686)

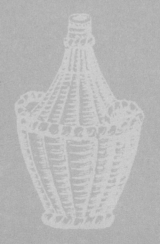

The Domesday Book from the late 11th century records vineyards in 46 places in southern England, increasing to 139 vineyards in England and Wales during the reign of Henry VIII, 11 of which were held by the Crown, 67 by noble families and 52 by the church. Vineyards suffered a decline in number after the dissolution of the monasteries, while French wines were imported in greater numbers.

When James I planted his vineyard at Oatlands Park in Surrey in 1603, he instigated a revival in vineyard planting among the nobility. One of the most celebrated vineyards at this time was at Hatfield House in Hertfordshire, laid out in 1611 for Robert Cecil. It included a collection of around 30,000 French vines, presented by Mme de la Boderie, wife of a French government minister. It was part of a water garden comprising meandering channels of water which formed islands and peninsulas, emphasising the ornamental nature of the vineyard. In 1640 Thomas Fuller, in his *Worthies* (1640), described it as 'a place … where Nature by the midwifery of Art, is delivered of much pleasure', and John Evelyn, after a visit in 1643, noted in his diary 'the most considerable rarity besides the house … was the Garden & Vineyard rarely well water'd and plant'd'.

An uncommon sight in Britain today, a view eastwards over the vineyard from Denbies Hill on the Box Hill estate, Surrey.

The revival of the British vineyard

Few other references to domestic vineyards were recorded until the 18th century when, coinciding with the era of the Grand Tour to Italy, landowners looked to representations of landscapes from classical antiquity as an inspiration for their gardens back home. At Painshill Park in Surrey, the vineyards established by Charles Hamilton flourished. Records from 1750 show the vineyard was planted with six different grape cultivars which produced excellent sparkling wine, deceiving even the French ambassador into declaring it 'un vrai Champagne'. The vineyard had declined by the beginning of the 19th century but happily it was restored in 1992, providing once again a wonderful picture of a textured south-facing slope when viewed from the highest point in the park. Although modern trellising is used in most of the 1ha (2½ acres), the last three vines at the bottom of each row are grown on the historic single-pole system. The first full crop was harvested in 1998 from the Painshill vineyard and today sparkling wines produced from the same vines are sold in the estate shop.

In the late 19th century, the Marquis of Bute established a commercial vineyard at Castell Coch outside Cardiff in South Wales. The Marquess died in 1900 but the vineyard remained in operation until it was grubbed up during the First World War. It was not until the middle of the 20th century that vines were grown on a commercial scale in England once again when Sir Guy Salisbury Jones planted up a vineyard at Hambledon in Hampshire, closely followed by the vineyard at the Beaulieu Estate, also in Hampshire, owned by Lord Montague.

The first commercial vineyard on National Trust land was created in 1995 at Ickworth House in Suffolk by tenants Charles and Jillian Macready, who planted 1ha (2.5 acres) of the south-facing slope of the walled kitchen garden with vines. The intention was not to produce dessert grapes as were once grown there but a fine English wine. In 2011 the royal household raised the profile still further by endorsing 3ha (7½ acres) of vineyards to be planted at Windsor Great Park. Although commercially managed, the project will be overseen by HRH the Duke of Edinburgh, giving the enterprise a royal seal of approval. The first vintage of sparkling white wine is expected in 2013. As with James I's venture in 1603, perhaps this enterprise will induce large estates to look to vineyards as a profitable and rewarding venture.

Grapes in one of the glasshouses at Tyntesfield, North Somerset.

ACKNOWLEDGEMENTS

The author would like to thank the following for their kind assistance, expertise and inspiration:

Christine Adams, Grant Berry, Mike Calnan, Bob Duff, Chris Gallagher, Peter Gammack, Susan Gronnow, Fiona Gunn, Eliza Lamb, Marian Mako, John and Rosa Morling, Professor Timothy Mowl, Tom and Sally North, Kristy Richardson, Tina Persaud, Cathy Gosling, Diana Vowles, Rosamund Saunders, Sally Bond, Laura Brodie, Peter Rolfe, Margaret Ann Stone, Professor Mark Stoyle and Michael Richardson. A special thank you to Kate Hughes, fellow garden historian and food enthusiast for her help and advice throughout.

CREDITS

Page 17 Private Collection/ Peter Newark Historical Pictures/ The Bridgeman Art Library; Page 23 Private Collection/ The Bridgeman Art Library; Page 40 The Stapleton Collection/ The Bridgeman Art Library; Page 71 © Samuel Courtauld Trust, The Courtauld Gallery, London, UK/ The Bridgeman Art Library; Page 79 Falmouth Art Gallery, Cornwall, UK/ The Bridgeman Art Library; Page 95 Private Collection/ The Stapleton Collection/ The Bridgeman Art Library; Page 96 Bibliotheque des Arts Decoratifs, Paris, France/ Archives Charmet/ The Bridgeman Art Library; Page 106 British Library, London, UK/ © British Library Board. All Rights Reserved/ The Bridgeman Art Library; Page 146 Berko Fine Paintings, Knokke-Zoute, Belgium/ The Bridgeman Art Library

Page 23 University of Bristol Library Special Collections

Page 68 and 157 © Country Life

Page 89 David Hosking/FLPA; Page 123 Hugh Clark/FLPA; Page 178 Marcel van Kammen/Minden Pictures/FLPA

Artwork pages 48, 51, 84, 109, 150, 151 and 152 by Alan Hancocks

Page 21, 42, 62, 89, 94, 98, 119, 121, 122, 137, 147, 167 Mary Evans Picture Library; Page 14, 28, 55 Interfoto/Mary Evans; Page 10 Retrograph/Mary Evans

Page 6, 43, 77, 124, 128, 131 © National Trust Images; Page 113 © National Trust Images/ Dudmaston, the Labouchere Collection (The National Trust); Page 171 © National Trust Images/NaturePL/Terry

Andrewartha; Page 181 © National Trust Images/Matthew Antrobus; Page 144 © National Trust Images/Cristian Barnett; Page 11, 46, 70, 72 © National Trust Images/Mark Bolton; Page 78 and 92 © National Trust Images/Jonathan Buckley; Page 36, 52, 64, 107, 114, 129, 135, 154, 188 © National Trust Images/Andrew Butler; Page 12, 35, 76 © National Trust Images/Neil Campbell-Sharp; Page 166 © National Trust Images/Colin Clarke; Page 50 and 169 © National Trust Images/Joe Cornish; Page 56 and 182 © National Trust Images/David Dixon; Page 156, 158, 160, 162, 163, 180, 185, 186 © National Trust Images/Andreas von Einsiedel; Page 183 © National Trust Images/Mark Fiennes; Page 125 © National Trust Images/Roy Fox; Page 176 © National Trust Images/Nick Garbutt; Page 60 © National Trust Images/Dennis Gilbert; Page 4, 13, 31, 38, 41, 74, 124, 143, 165, 172, 173, 174, 175, 177, 187 © National Trust Images/John Hammond; Page 86 © NT/E.Chambré Hardman Collection; Page 9, 15, 22, 24, 44, 45, 57, 66, 85, 108 © National Trust Images/Paul Harris; Page 130 © National Trust Images/Andrew Haslam; Page 77, 91, 93, 99, 111 © National Trust Images /Ross Hoddinott; Page 118 © National Trust Images/Angelo Hornak; Page 126 © National Trust Images/Christopher Hurst; Page 37, 61, 63 © National Trust Images/Andrea Jones; Page 102 and 133 © National Trust Images/David Levenson; Page 159 © National Trust Images/Nadia Mackenzie; Page 127 © National Trust Images/Leo Mason; Page 67, 110, 132, 148, 184 © National Trust Images/John Millar; Page 87 © National Trust Images /Paul Mogford; Page 145 © National Trust Images/Andrew Montgomery; Page 104 © National Trust Images/Geoff Morgan; Page

58, 83, 115, 161, 174 © National Trust Images/Robert Morris; Page 112 © National Trust Images/David Noton; Page 7, 16, 20, 25, 29, 47, 53, 55, 59, 73, 81, 90, 117, 189 © National Trust Images/Stephen Robson; Page 19 and 109 © National Trust Images/ David Sellman; Page 116 © National Trust Images/Arnhel de Serra; Page 2, 33, 138 © National Trust Images/Ian Shaw; Page 26 and 82 © National Trust Images/William Shaw; Page 164 © National Trust Images/Megan Taylor; Page 54 © National Trust Images/Robert Thrift; Page 136 © National Trust Images/Rupert Truman; Page 155 © National Trust Images/Charlie Waite; Page 80 © National Trust Images/Paul Wakefield; Page 134 © National Trust Images/Mike Williams; Page 179 © National Trust Images/J. Whitaker; Page 8, 30, 140 © National Trust Images/Derrick E. Witty

Page 141 The Royal Collection © 2011 Her Majesty Queen Elizabeth II

Page 139 by kind permission of the Duke of Beaufort

Page 100 by kind permission of Lambton Estates

Page 34 by kind permission of Nicky Brent, The Sanctuary, Shobrooke, Devon. Photograph by Peter Gammack

Page 65 and 105 photograph by Peter Gammack

Page 39 photograph by Amy Forster

Extract from Food In England by Dorothy Hartley, published by Piatkus. Copyright © 1945 by Dorothy Hartley. Reproduced by permission of Sheil Land Associates Ltd

BIBLIOGRAPHY

Anon, *Sketches of Rural Affairs*, (London, 1851)

Arnold, Dana, The Georgian Country House, (Sutton Publishing, 2003)

Aston, David, and Bucknall, Sally, *Plants and Honey Bees, their Relationships*, (Northern Bee Books, 2009)

Atkyns, Sir Robert, *The Ancient and Present State of Gloucestershire*, (London 1708)

Austin, Jane, *Pride and Prejudice*, (Oxford University Press, 1986)

Bacon, Francis, *Essays*, (J.M. Dent, 1999)

Baker, Margaret, *Discovering the Folklore of Plants*, (Shire Publications Ltd., 2005)

Bamford, Francis, ed., *A Royalist's Notebook, The Commonplace Book of Sir John Oglander, 1622-1652*, (Constable & Co Ltd. 1936)

Batey, Mavis., Lambert, David, *The English Garden Tour*, (John Murray, 1990)

Beeton, Isabella, *The Book of Household Management, 1861*, (Wordsworth Additions, 2006)

Biggs, Matthew, Jekka McVicar, Flowerdew, Bob, *Vegetables, Herbs & Fruit* (Silverdale books, 2003)

Bown, Deni, *RHS Encyclopedia of Herbs and their Uses*, (Dorling Kindersley, 1995)

Brown, Ron, *Beekeeping, a Seasonal Guide*, (Batsford, 2011)

Bushnell, Rebecca, *Green Desire, Imagining Early Modern English Gardens*, (Cornell University Press, 2003)

Buxbaum, Tim, *Icehouses*, (Shire Publications, 2008)

Byng, John, *The Torrington Diaries*, ed. Bruyn Andrews, C., 4 vols., (Methuen & Co. 1970)

Campbell, Susan, *A History of Kitchen Gardening*, (Francis Lincoln, 2005)

Castelvetro, Giacomo, *The Fruit, Herbs and Vegetables of Italy*, (Viking, 1989)

Clifford, Sue and King, Angela, *The Apple Source Book*, (Hodder & Stoughton, 2007)

Collins Beekeeper's Bible, (Harper Collins 2010)

Colquhoun, Kate, *Taste, the Story of Britain through its Cooking*, (Bloomsbury, 2007)

Colvin, Howard and Newman, Johns, (eds), *Of Building: Roger North's Writings on Architecture* (Oxford, Clarendon Press, 1981)

Culpeper, Nicholas, *Culpeper's Complete Herbal*, (Arcturus Publishing Ltd., 2009)

Currie, Christopher K., 'Fishponds as Garden Features c.1550-1750,' *The Journal of the Garden History Society*, 18:1 (Spring 1990)

Davidson, Alan, *The Oxford Companion to Food*, (Oxford University Press, 2006)

Dawson, Mark, *Plenti and Grase, Food and Drink in a Sixteenth-Century Household*, (Prospect Books, 2009)

Day, Ivan, *Ice Cream*, (Shire Publications Ltd., 2011)

Defoe, Daniel, *The Compleat English Gentleman*, c.1728, (Pub. David Nutt, 1890)

Defoe, Daniel, *A Tour through the Whole of the Island of Great Britain*, ed. Cole, G.D.H., 4 Vols, (Folio Society, 1983)

Downing, Mr, 'A Picture of a Nobleman's Seat', *The Horticulturalist* vol. V (Oct 1850)

Eastoe, Jane, *Henkeeping*, (National Trust Books, 2007)

Eburne, Andrew, 'The Passion of Sir Thomas Tresham: New Light on the Gardens and Lodge at Lyveden', *The Journal of the Garden History Society*, 36:1 (Summer 2008)

Ellis, William, *The Country Housewife's Family Companion*, (1750)

Evelyn, John, *The Diary and Correspondence of John Evelyn*, ed. Bray, William, 4 vols., (Hurst and Blackett, 1854)

Evelyn, John, *Directions for the Gardener and other Horticultural Advice*, ed., Campbell-Culver, Maggie, (Oxford University Press, 2009)

Evelyn, John, *Acetaria, A Discourse of Sallets*, 1699, (Prospect Books, 2005)

Evans, George Ewart, *Ask the Fellows who Cut the Hay*, (Full Circle Editions, 2010)

Exwood, Maurice, and Lehmann, H. L., *The Journal of William Schellinks' Travels in England, 1661-1663*, (Royal Historical Society, 1993)

Farrar, Linda, *Ancient Roman Gardens* (Sutton Publishing Ltd., 1998)

Fearnley-Whittingstall, Jane, *The Garden an English Love affair*, (Weidenfeld & Nicholson, 2002)

Felus, Kate, 'Boats and Boating in the Designed lasndscape', *The Journal of the Garden History Society*, 34:1 (Summer 2006)

Fletcher, John, *Gardens of Earthly Delight, the History of Deer Parks*, (Windgather Press, 2011)

Flowerdew, Bob, *The Companion Garden*, (Kyle Cathie, 1994)

Gallagher, Christopher, 'Paradise Lost and Regained', *The National Trust Arts, Buildings, Collections Bulletin*, (July 2009)

Gordon, Catherine, *Coventrys of Croome*, (Phillimore & Co Ltd., 2000)

Grigson, Jane, *Food with the Famous*, (Grub Street, 1991)

Grigson, Sophie, and Black, William, *Fish*, (Headline Book Publishing, 2000)

Foster, A.M, *Bee Boles and Bee Houses*, (Shire Publications Ltd., 2010)

Hansell, Peter & Jean, *Dovecotes*, (Shire Publications Ltd., 2001)

Hardyment, Christina, *Behind the Scenes, Domestic arrangements in Historic Houses*, (National Trust, 1997)

Harris, John, Jackson-Stops, Gervase, eds., *Britannia Illustrata*, (Paradigm Press 1984)

Hart-Davis, Duff, *Fauna Britannica*, (Weidenfeld & Nicholson, 2002)

Hartley, Dorothy, *Food in England*, (Macdonald, 1954)

Harvey, John H., 'Vegetables in the Middle Ages', *The Journal of the Garden History Society*, 12:2 (Autumn 1984)

Henderson, Paula, *The Tudor House and Garden* (Yale, 2005)

Hibbert, Christopher, *The English, a Social History 1066-1945*, (Harper Collins, 1994)

Hooper, Ted, *Guide to Bees and Honey*, (Northern Bee Books, 2010)

Hunt, John Dixon, *Andrew Marvell, His Life and Writings*, (Elek Books, 2007)

James, John, *The Theory and Practice of Gardening*, 1712, (Gregg International Publishers Ltd., 1969)

Jellicoe, Geoffrey and Susan, Goode, Patrick, and Lancaster, Michael, *The Oxford Companion to Gardens*, (Oxford Universtiy Press, 2001)

Klein, Carol, *Grow Your Own Fruit*, (Mitchell Beazley, 2009)

Langley, Batty, *New Principles of Gardening*, 1728, (Gregg International Publishers Ltd., 1971)

Larkcom, Joy, *Creative Vegetable Gardening*, (Mitchell Beazley, 2004)

Lasdun, Susan, *English Park: Royal, Private and Public*, (Andre Deutsch, 1991)

Lawson, William, *A New Orchard and Garden with The Country Housewifes Garden*, 1618, (Prospect Books, 2003)

Loudon, Jane *The Lady's Country Companion*, 1845, (Paradigm Press, 1984)

Markham Gervase, *The English Husbandman*, 1613 (Garland publishing, 1982)

May, Robert, *The Accomplisht Cook*, 1664 (Prospect Books, 1994)

McMorland Hunter, Jane, and Kelly, Chris, *For the Love of an Orchard*, (Pavilion, 2010)

McVicar, Jekka, *Good Enough to Eat*, (Kyle Cathie Ltd., 1997)

Morgan, Joan, & Richards, Alison, *The New Book of Apples* (Ebury Press, 2002)

Morris, Christopher, (ed.), *The Illustrated Journeys of Celia Fiennes*, (Webb and Bower, 1982)

Mowl, Timothy, *Historic Gardens of England: Gloucestershire*, (Tempus Publishing, 2002)

Mowl, Timothy and Mako, Marion, *Historic Gardens of England: Cheshire*, (Redcliffe Press, 2008)

North, Roger, *A Discourse of Fish and Fishponds*, (London, 1713)

North, Roger, *Memoirs of Norths*, 3 vols. (Henry Colburn, 1826)

Paston-Williams, Sara, *The Art of Dining*, (National Trust, 1999)

Peachey, Stuart, *The Edgehill Campaign and the Letters of Nehemiah Wharton* (Partizan Press, 1997)

Peters, J. E. C., *Discovering Traditional Farm Buildings*, (Shire Publications Ltd., 2003)

Peterson, T. Sarah, *The Cookbook that Changed the World: the Origins of Modern Cuisine*, (Tempus publishing, 2006)

Pettitt, Elizabeth L., *Clwyd Archives Cookbook*, (Clwyd Record Office, 1980)

Phillips, Roger, *Wild Food*, (Pan Books Ltd., 1983)

Plaw, John, *Ferme Ornée or Rural Improvements*, (Gregg International Publishers, 1972)

Roberts, Jane, *Royal Palaces, The Gardens and Parks of Windsor*, (Yale University Press, 1997)

Roberts, Judith, 'Well Temper'd Clay: Constructing Water Features in the Landscape Park', *The Journal of the Garden History Society*, 29:1 (Summer 2001)

Robinson, John Martin, *The English Country Estate*, (National Trust, 1988)

Rolfe, Peter, *Crock of Gold, Seeking the Crucian Carp*, (M Press Ltd., 2010)

Russell, James, *Man-Made Eden, Historic Orchards in Somerset and Gloucestershire*, (Redcliffe Press, 2007)

Sambrook, Pamela, *A Country House at Work*, (National Trust, 2003)

Stevenson, Jane, Davidson, Peter, (eds) *The Closet of Sir Kenelm Digby Opened*, 1669 (Prospect Books, 2009)

Stocks, Christopher, *Forgotten Fruits*, (Random House, 2008)

Strong, Roy, *The Renaissance Garden in England*, (Thames and Hudson, 1998)

Strong, Roy, *The Artist and the Garden*, (Yale University Press, 2000)

Temple, William, *Upon the Gardens of Epicurus; or Of Gardening in the Year 1685*, (Pallas, 2004)

Thear, Katie, *Starting with Chickens*, (Broad Leas Publishing Ltd., 1999)

Tremlin, Betty, ' A Life Full of Horses', *DYDDI Digest 424* (January 2011)

Walker, Penelope, and Crane, Eva, 'The History of Beekeeping in English Gardens' *The Journal of the Garden History Society*, 28:2 (Winter 2000)

Walton, Izaak and Cotton, Charles, *The Complete Angler*, (Arcturus Publishing Ltd., 2010)

Warren, Piers, *How to Store your Garden Produce, the Key to Self-Sufficiency*, (Green Books, 2009)

Wentworth, Lady, *Recipe Book*, c.1730 (Manuscript, Dunham Massey)

Whittle, Elizabeth, and Taylor, Christopher, 'The early Seventeenth-Century Gardens of Tackley, Oxfordshire', *The Journal of the Garden History Society*, 22:1 (Summer 1994)

Williamson, Tom, *Suffolk's Gardens and Parks*, (Windgather Press, 2000)

Williamson, Tom, *The Archaeology of Rabbit Warrens*, (Shire Publications Ltd., 2006)

Wilson, C. Anne, (ed.), *The Country House Kitchen Garden*, (The History Press, 2010)

Woodforde, Rev. James, *The Diary of a Country Parson*, (Folio Society, 1992)

INDEX